WHAT YOUR HOROSCOPE DOESN'T TELL YOU

WHAT YOUR HOROSCOPE DOESN'T TELL YOU

CHARLES STROHMER

 Tyndale House
Publishers, Inc.
Wheaton, Illinois

All Scripture quotations are
from *The Holy Bible,* New
International Version, copyright 1978 by New York International Bible Society,
unless otherwise noted.

Second printing, November 1988

Library of Congress
Catalog Card Number
87-50995
ISBN 0-8423-7936-3
Copyright 1988 by Charles
R. Strohmer
All rights reserved
Printed in the United States
of America

To *SUE* and to *JIM*

CONTENTS

.

ONE
AFTER AQUARIUS

"The time has come," wrote astrologer Llewellyn George, "for the masses as a whole to take an interest in the subject."[1]

The subject was astrology, and he was writing in the 1930s. In an era when people were becoming fascinated by technology and new discoveries in the physical sciences, George's words must have seemed out of step, perhaps even backward. Now it's clear he was ahead of his time.

Astrology mushroomed in the 1960s and 1970s. A rock musical heralded the dawning of the "Age of Aquarius." As young people and the culture they pioneered went after Eastern religions, drug trips, and all sorts of new experiences, astrology gained immense popularity. Today the fad has become a foothold. Astrology is without doubt the most acceptable occult pastime of our age. It has become an unquestionable part of everyday life.

Astrology is big business getting bigger. Thousands of newspapers carry daily horoscope columns. Bumper stickers and license plates proudly proclaim one's allegiance to Scorpio, Leo, or Aries. Judging from the rife sales of astrological computer calculators, chart vending machines, textbooks, paperback guides, trinkets, and the like, we fool ourselves if we think that astrology is passé.

I studied and practiced astrology myself in the late 1960s and early 1970s, constructing horoscopes for various clients. I found the response overwhelmingly favorable toward the craft. Whether I was in Boston, Detroit, Chicago, Los Angeles, or smaller stops in between, few were the people who did not have a good appetite for this religion-science.

Yet, one thing annoyed me. Whenever someone did speak out against the craft, he would speak antagonistically instead of authoritatively. A typical counterstatement went about as far as, "You're not into that garbage, are you?" Or, "What do you want to get involved with that nonsense for?" In such a person's eyes I was as alien as if I had actually come from one of the planets that I talked so much about.

In a way, I was comforted by this. *They don't know what they're talking about,* I thought. *Most critics of astrology have never read a serious book on the subject, or attended lectures, or actually erected and delineated a chart. So, what can such critics know?* I knew that astrology's most zealous opponents were usually those who had never studied the craft in depth. Thus their arguments were based on ignorance and showed me no good reason to stop studying. So I kept at it. Sometimes things would become so intense that I would wrestle with the craft for hours a day, day after day, laboring over various texts and charts. I would dig deeper and deeper, trying to discover astrology's secrets and how I thought it worked. And I tried to keep an open mind, thinking, *If this is nonsense, or perhaps just wrong, why can't someone tell me why?*

Like you, I know what it is to try to track down truth. It's frustrating. Just when you think you have it, it darts off like a wet watermelon seed that you try to trap between the tabletop and your thumb. Time and time again this phenomenon occurs in astrology. Astrology books are silent as to why this is so. Regarding this crucial point, we have not been treated fairly by astrological literature. It may come as surprising to you, but some vital facts concerning astrology are either left out of the texts or concealed. Apart from them we cannot determine exactly what astrology is. That may explain why the truth of it escapes at the last second.

The difficult things ahead that have to be said, I have tried to say sensitively and simply, though firmly. I have written for anyone who has heard the words *astrology* or *horoscope,* whether yours is the fleeting interest of the passerby or the deepening commitment of a disciple, whether you read newspaper horoscopes occasionally or have published books on the subject. I have tried to begin on the ground shared by everyone who, at the least, knows his or her sun-sign, and then unpack a few areas of the craft that are not openly discussed in astrology books themselves. This is not a traditional look at astrology; it is the beginning of a redefinition of it.

Because of the craft's popularity, I did not think it necessary to describe much about what its books say about the basics. What is necessary is that we skim off the meringue from the top of the pie, scoop out the lemon, break open the crust, and analyze some of the essential ingredients of this particular pie— before biting. We might decide not to eat.

This little book does not argue from a standpoint of ignorance. As much as a person can be, I was into astrology for almost eight years. And I stayed with it because it "worked." I thought that this was a good enough reason to stick with something. In July 1976 I found out that this was not reason enough. This may seem obvious, but not until then did I grasp that just because something "works," it is not necessarily synonymous with what is right and true. That a thing works does not mean that it should be used. Some things when they work explode and maim.

If astrology works, *why* does it work? *How* does it work? If it has power or knowledge, *where* does it come from? And why are some crucial details packed away in silence, so that we are presented with a picture of the astrological heavens other than the one we should have? These are the questions that astrological literature avoids. I'd like to consider them in this little book.

TWO
ASTROLOGY'S APPEAL

Phyllis could have been your child. She could have been your best friend, or your neighbor, one of the many fascinated by astrology. She came to me during the peak of my astrological career, in 1974. She was a pleasant young woman, in her late twenties, and she was searching for answers. After overhearing her boyfriend speak about me, she decided to have her horoscope done.

Many years have passed since the night Phyllis and I sat at her dining room table and I read her horoscope. Yet I remember that evening vividly, especially the thrill of being able to discern in her horoscope some events from her past. I saw things about Phyllis that I had no previous knowledge of. Discerning these, I was then able to talk to her about them. This is quite a startling and catchy phenomenon. Phyllis knew that I did not know about these events, and I knew that I did not. Yet here the horoscope was disclosing specific episodes from out of her past. How almost hypnotic the evening became, persuading us both to deepen our interest in the subject: me as a teacher, her as a now less skeptical observer. We will come back to Phyllis in a later chapter. But if she were your daughter, how would you approach her new interest in the subject?

Or consider my friend Skip. Because Skip and I traveled together for a year, working as repairmen for a glass company, we spent hours airing the pros and cons surrounding astrology. I usually tried to convert him, but he never quite bought it. One weekend Skip had to fly home to Michigan— we were working in Massachusetts—for the funeral of someone I'll call Al. I asked Skip to bring back Al's time, place, and date of birth. With those ingredients I could erect the birth horoscope (called a birth chart or a natal chart) of the deceased and compare it with a horoscope of the day he died (called a progressed chart). With these two charts I could determine, astrologically, why he had died when he did. To smoke out this answer, I needed to know what "planetary influences" contributed to his death.

Skip returned and I cast the two required charts. Late into the night, in our room at the Holiday Inn, we discussed what I saw as certain, clear reasons for the death—that is, major, "adverse" planetary influences that spoke of death showed up in both charts. For a long time Skip and I talked about these influences. We finally agreed that my conclusions could not be proven. But the phenomenon we experienced was still enticing. The question is, What do you say to your neighbor, Skip, when he is back in Michigan telling you about this remarkable night he spent deep in thought and talk about these astrological indications?

For Phyllis, Skip, and countless others, astrology is not just something people are wearing around the necks or sticking on their car bumpers. It is something to be interested in, to follow, to depend upon, and to look to for answers. Fifty or sixty years ago there was little need to have a manageable understanding of the religion-science of astrology. It was rare to meet those who took the craft seriously. Today that has changed.

Why has the absorption of astrology into the soul of our society, whether in the fleeting curiosity of the passersby or in the deepening commitment of its disciples, been so thorough? $ $ $ $ $. There is money to be made. Many privateers use astrology as a gimmick, to filch a Hamilton from your wallet. Newspaper horoscopes, sun-sign and love-sign paperbacks, and all the astrological knickknacks and chart vending machines have turned astrology into a pop object. And there is money in pop objects.

But what is the appeal? Nothing sells well if people don't like it. Well, it's fun. There are other, deeper reasons, which we'll get to, but on the surface astrology seems like harmless fun. It shows its participants another world, like that of *Star Wars* or *The Hobbit*, the world of the stars. That world has its rules and rulers, its forces, its characters, even its own kind of language or code. It's a game, in a way, and many are "just playing."

Another reason for the mass interest in astrology is its view of human nature: it seems to instruct on matters of the soul without being morally demanding. It claims to explain quirks of our personalities and tell us whether to pursue love or money today, but requires nothing of us morally. And we like this. Our society isn't much interested in moral blueprints. We want to decide for ourselves what is right or wrong, good or bad, true or false, without any outside interference. Scrap the Ten Commandments. In this era we rush to methodologies, like astrology, that simply give out information about human nature yet require no moral obligation from us. Astrology has risen today because it offers information about the universe and the soul, and yet it contains no fixed moral framework to which we must commit ourselves.

Astrology is also popular because it works. An astrologer's delineations can be astonishingly accurate, disclosing personal facts about the client or recounting actual events from the client's past. These self-disclosures reinforce people's interest in the system. Everyone likes to know more about himself, what makes him tick. But people aren't stupid. Methodologies that continually bungle at disclosing information seldom thrive. Such *mis*information never stimulates trust. Astrology thrives, in part, because of its accurate self-disclosures.

Yet note carefully: astrological self-disclosures are of a totally different nature from those we normally think of, as from a counselor or an M.D. In a relationship between a patient and a psychiatrist, the patient unloads hours of information about himself upon his psychiatrist. The psychiatrist in turn tallies up all this shared data and, hopefully, comes up with significant self-disclosures regarding the patient. The point is that the detailed self-disclosures result directly from the patient's hours of conversation with the psychiatrist.

Astrological self-disclosures are reached differently. Clients do not need to discuss previously any personal information with their astrologers. They can receive detailed information (self-disclosures) about themselves even if they have never previously conversed with their astrologers. This is, indeed, a startling and catchy phenomenon. The client's time, place, and date of birth (ingredients necessary to erect a horoscope) are the only prior pieces of information needed by a seasoned astrologer in order to self-disclose to a client. It is not that clients do not chat with their astrologers. They do. But that is not a prerequisite for astrological self-disclosures. The astrologer simply needs to have one's chart and to know how to interpret it.

Astrological self-disclosures expose the details, the particulars, of one's personal life. In one's horoscope, an astrologer may discover that his client broke her arm in the fifth grade, or that she won a lottery four years ago, or that her violent temper cost her two years in prison. Notice the emphasis on details (not generalities): broken arm—fifth grade; lottery—four years; violent temper—prison—two years. This remarkable phenomenon of self-disclosure inspires the masses, who want to know more about themselves, to trust in the system.

It isn't that everyone in the country has personally experienced these self-disclosures. But many have heard stories of them. A friend of mine once attended a public meeting where an astrologer was speaking. This astrologer had, in front of her, many of the horoscopes of those gathered in that room, persons she had never met. The astrologer chose my friend's horoscope and saw from reading it that my friend was small-boned, which she is. How could the astrologer know this detail without seeing this woman? The self-disclosure caught everyone's attention. I cannot think of anyone, myself included, who became less interested in astrology after experiencing or even just hearing about self-disclosures. And the word spreads. We will look at this phenomenon in depth in chapter 7.

There is yet a fourth reason—other than money and fun, the lack of moral principles, and the luxury of self-disclosures—that accounts for the craft's acceptance today.

And this is no small matter. The religion-science of astrology must not reveal only details on the surface of human nature, it must speak to issues beneath. It must furnish answers for our underlying, what we might call our spiritual, needs and hopes. Besides being relativistic and autonomous, our age is quickly realizing the shallowness of collecting material possessions. As our affluence leaves us unfulfilled, we are becoming desperate for answers that will satisfy our underlying spiritual needs. We are becoming searchers for answers to the big questions of life. And, again, we are not ignorant. We will not settle for any answer; we want *the* answers. We desire *authentic answers* to the underlying big questions:

What is reality?

Who am I? What am I doing here?

Is there a God? Or some kind of governing force to the universe?

I'm just dead after I die . . . right?

Sin? Forgiveness? Jesus?

There's no heaven or hell . . . is there?

Is the Bible true? What about the Koran, or Buddhism?

We have honest questions. These are some of the big ones. Beyond the mere fun and fascination, many turn to astrology because they believe they will find spiritual help there.

A word about authentic answers.

Persons who honestly search for spiritual truth do so because of a spiritual hunger. They often notice in themselves an unrelenting tug pulling them onward, no matter what the cost, to get the big questions answered. I can tell you that this necessary tugging will continue until *authentic answers* are discovered *and* accepted. Only then will this pesky disturbance in the heart be permanently quieted and satisfied, and you will know it. Only *authentic answers* hold the special power to quiet the unrelenting annoyance generated by the big questions remaining unanswered. In them alone are hidden the treasures of spiritual truth. Authentic answers are those answers that truly decode our dilemmas about ourselves, the mysteries of the universe, and the nature of God.

I will have more to say about authentic answers later. Yet many turn to astrology, failing to discover authentic answers in other methodologies, hoping that it will impart these answers. I know that the latitude of the astrological heavens seems to set forth the best possible spiritual answers. When eyes, however, rise to the Zodiac, there comes a risk. And every time you crack its books or delineate a chart, you run that risk. Is it an authentic answer? Does it *truly* decode the big questions? Is there even a way to tell?

THREE
LET THE GODS SPEAK

Perhaps you are only casually interested. Treating your horoscope like a Chinese fortune cookie, you match its speculations
to the specifics of your life—and laugh with recognition when it
fits. Perhaps you take the horoscope's broad advice—"Make
friends with a stranger," "Write to a distant friend." No harm in
that, is there? Perhaps you just wear a bracelet or carry a key
chain with an emblem of your sun-sign. It's an ID of sorts,
marking when you were born. Perhaps you find the Zodiac an
interesting conversation piece—"What's your sign?" Or perhaps you have even had your chart done. A friend says, "You're
an Aquarius, aren't you? An Aquarius is like that," and she's
right. Then she begs you to let her do your horoscope. So you
give in. Why not? Can't hurt, right? You might even learn something about yourself.

Even if your interest is superficial, perhaps you would think
twice if you realized that when you turn to astrology you are
actually turning to advice from the ancient gods of a peculiar
polytheistic religion. Oh, astrology sounds very scientific; its
books are well-stocked with references to planets and stars. But
as you look deeper into its texts, you realize it's not the *planets*
you're interpreting, it's the *gods they're named after.* Saturn,
for instance, is said to affect people in a constricting, malevolent
way. But these are not the characteristics of the planet—that's
just a big sphere with rings around it—it's the god Saturn from

ancient Roman mythology who was revered as a threatening and sinister primeval power.

Yet astrologers continually cite "planetary" influences as being at work in human affairs. They do not cite "the gods." This is because all astrology books are outfitted in *planetary* nomenclature. Llewellyn George wrote in his *A to Z Horoscope Maker and Delineator:* "Astrology is taken from the records of astral phenomena and reduced to a science by observing the effects of *planetary* influence. . . . More is now known about *planetary* influence and human response."[2] In Margaret E. Hone's *Modern Textbook of Astrology* we read: "Astrology is a unique system of interpretation of the correlation of *planetary* action in human experience."[3] (Italics mine.) Elsewhere, George states that one should not shoulder off responsibility on a *planet* but, on the contrary, learn by *planetary* indications. These statements about the planets are typical throughout astrological literature. It is as though the reader is being educated about the planets of our solar system. But astrology is not astronomy.

To the astronomer, of course, Mercury, Venus, Mars, Jupiter, Saturn, Uranus, Neptune, and Pluto are names of planets, but to the astrologer that list is a titanic collection of legends and myths. Astrology takes elements of astronomy and steeps them in ancient Greek and Roman mythology. The system is based not on the physical properties of the planets but on the distinctives, attributes, and desperate limitations of each god in the closed circle of astrological polytheism.

If this were an astrology book, most of its pages would elaborate the characteristics of the gods, how they differ, and how their natures do or do not mix. Here is a brief sampling. The books portray Jupiter's nature as expansive, good-willed, benefic; he represents success in finances. Saturn, as was mentioned, is to be understood in sharp antithesis: constricting, binding, malefic. Venus influences the higher attributes of a person, that is, writing, drama, the arts, music. Mars affects athletic ability and is said to govern wars. Neptune's influence is said to be more psychic than physical. Pluto is said to rule the world of the abode of the dead. And on and on the stories go. Whole chapters are devoted to just one god. Principles of astrological interpretation are clearly excerpted from ancient myths, updated, and have absolutely nothing to do with planets but with superstitions and imaginings relating to mythical deities. This literature, therefore, should not use the material word *planet* because in fact the studies bear upon the elaborately devised intrigue of the gods.

In science class we are taught about planets. In science class it is right. In astrology it is wrong. Astrologers are not astronomers. In the rationale of astrology, "gods" are assigned control over different parts of the human anatomy and over different spheres of human activity and personality. This should be clearly indicated throughout astrological literature. But it is concealed.

This misuse of terms is responsible for gross misunderstandings. The idea that the planets influence our lives is a major astrological pillar, perhaps *the* major one. Yet, principles of planetary influences can be preached only at the expense of truth; for the twist of nomenclature hides what actually constitutes this pillar: the gods. Thus, the writings communicate a false impression—that the planets of our solar system influence our lives.

From what we have just unpacked, we see the clear evidence that it is the *gods* (not planets) that influence our lives. This is what the texts would have to say if they were honest with us. What immediately follows from this is almost unbelievable, especially to the person who has been into astrology for a time. Because this major pillar consists of imaginary gods and their mythical principles, this adds up to the embarrassing conclusion that what I have been leaning on is not even there! And the fall is damaging. The major astrological pillar, in which I have been trusting, is imaginary. It does not exist. To anyone who has been seriously interested in astrology this, at first, seems incredible. It is mind-altering to realize now that there is no such thing, astrologically, as a planetary influence. Yet that is the truth. We do not inbreathe mythological influences at birth; we inbreathe air.

In fairness, it must be noted that some pioneer astrologers, like Llewellyn George, do admit a minor distinction between the physical mass of a planet and what they call a "life within." When George writes that astrology may be considered *objective* because it deals with the outer expression of other worlds, he also states that "astrology may be considered *subjective,* dealing with the influence of the *life within the form*"[4] (italics mine). He tags the mythical god-knowledge as an influencing life within the form of a planet. Yet, though he discriminates between the planet's form and a supposed life within, he and his peers avoid using the correct term (god) to identify this supposed life and influence. This is inherent misinformation.

An astrologer has only one use for the actual planets. He uses them to erect the charts (horoscopes). For this mathematical task he needs an ephemeris. This is a book used by astronomers. It lists the coordinates of the planets, in their orbits, during specific times of the year. Once an astrologer has used the ephemeris to locate the planets and construct the chart, his studies from then on bear upon the gods.

All of this should create some second thoughts. Despite the scientific language of astrology, you are really wading into a religion. Suddenly, you're not just splashing in harmless fun; it's serious business. There is generally only room for one religion in each soul; you had better choose yours with care.

So when you check your daily horoscope and it tells you that the location of Mars in your chart (the planet is present in the sky and somehow the characteristics of the god are supposed to be present in your life) indicates that you will have a fight with someone—and this in fact comes to pass—you have two ways to interpret that:

1. It's a coincidence. But then why do you keep checking your horoscope? To find another coincidence. And if you find enough coincidences, it's no longer coincidence, is it? The very laws of probability demand some cause for the horoscope's repeated accuracy (if indeed you find it accurate), some force or power that brings about those events.

It may be coincidence—but your continued dabbling in it betrays your suspicion that it may be more. If astrology does not correspond to reality at all, if the foretold events never actually happen, then the whole thing is a pointless exercise and kind of boring. Coincidences, however, piled together, may tip the balance toward the second interpretation, though you may not want to admit it.

2. There is power in astrology (though we have just seen that it is not in the planets). But if you choose this view, suddenly you're not a dabbler anymore, you're becoming a devotee. And

now you're presented with another set of choices you may not have considered:

a. The religion of astrology is true; its power, whatever it is, is good. In order for this to work, astrology has to give you the authentic answers to the big questions. But we have already noted the *false* explanation of its major pillar, planetary influence. That in itself should make us at least seriously consider a second choice.

b. It's a false religion. It has power, but the power is deceptive. In this case, it is nothing to toy with.

c. Unfortunately, many refuse to choose (a) or (b). They think they are neither in nor out, but holding astrology at arm's length. The power in it attracts them, but they don't stop to consider whether it's right or wrong. They want to believe in an astrology that's benign. They won't demand authentic answers from it, just a little amazement every so often. And they never think about the power behind it or the demands *it* may make of *them.*

We'll deal with this further in a later chapter. But now let's consider options (a) and (b). Is astrology reliable? Or is it false religion?

FOUR
IS IT RELIABLE?

Our first clue about the reliability of astrology comes in the area of integrity. Does it mean what it says? We have just seen that astrology talks about "planets" when it really means "gods." Now there is a great difference between a thing that is real (a planet) and a thing that is imaginary (a god). Except for their names being the same, there is no similarity at all. Yet by its literary metamorphosis of "god" into "planet," astrology subtly indoctrinates us into believing that we are being taught about the bodily details of the physical forms, and how they affect us, while we are actually absorbing imaginary ideas about mythical deities. Practically, out on the street, where things are real and where we hurt for answers, we are asked to turn for help to that which—unknown to us—is not real, to that which is imaginary, to that which has no life. Astrology is intellectually abusive at this point; it perverts one's thinking. At this point, the system lacks the integrity of authentic answers.

Yet this error not only sidetracks the individual mind; it warps a whole society's thinking. Since both astrologer and client are trained to *think planet,* they *talk planet.* This comes naturally. In answers to a client's query, one never hears an astrologer respond, "Well, you have this god in the sixth house." Or, "You have these three gods in a trine." Rather, the conditioned response is, "You have Mercury in the sixth house." Or, "You have no aspects to this planet." One problem with this is that, in all public conversations like this, the concealment, misunderstanding, and misinformation concerning this major astrological pillar is carried further and further out into the culture. People are spreading myths, basing their lives on them, and it goes unnoticed because they think and talk in a planetary nomenclature. People are basing their lives on myths while assuming that they are learning and leaning upon something real! It goes unnoticed because continually hearing the words *planet* and *planetary* creates a connotation of real-ness. The imaginary-ness of what is behind what is being said is overlooked. It is covered up.

No one is going to deny that the planet Jupiter is there. It is an awesome mass of reality. In astrology, when Jupiter or Mars or Uranus is mentioned, one gets the picture of large physical masses twirling around the sun. There is a definite solidness about them that comes to mind. Astrologically, though, this real-ness is only a mirage. It is a fake image, because the astrology books are really talking about the gods, not the planets. People receive a connotation of real-ness regarding something from which they should receive a definite awareness of something imaginary.

Why do the books cover up what is essential to correct knowledge? What is at stake here is mental soundness, and not only on an individual basis. To be sincere is not necessarily to be correct. Even if I am sincerely dedicated to the sun as being cold, the stars as black points in the night sky, and the moon as a green square, I am wrong. I am not sound. I need help. What if a whole culture develops such blurred thinking?

For some reason, astrology books do not want us to see clearly. They want to hide the fact that they are placing the false gods of a polytheistic religion before us. They don't want our consciences to have to deal with the moral problem of allegiance to false gods. This notion may seem antiquated and irrelevant for our relativistic age today; nevertheless, it is relevant for knowing the truth and acting upon what is right. For truth is right. And truth has power—power to nudge us, through our consciences, away from what is false, wrong, and harmful. Try the simple experiment of replacing the terms "planetary" and "planet" with the terms "the gods'" and "gods" in the quotes in the previous chapter. A little bell should ring when I read that I should not shoulder off responsibility to a *god* but learn by the *gods'* indications; or, that more is now known about the *gods'* influence and human response.

It would be hard to prove whether the error in nomenclature, and the subsequent harm caused by it, is intentional. Whether calculated or not, it is a deception. One might ask, therefore, "Would the correction of terms give value to this major astrological pillar? Would the tenets, then, be substantial and profitable? Could we lean on them?" The answer is no. Even if astrology came to honest terms with itself, and us, we would nonetheless hear in these tenets the same voice: myth. In the literature of mythical principles, whether called gods, planets, or whatever, we hear a voice that at best is mythological.

And this is our second clue against the reliability of astrology. Not only does it misname the basic elements of its system, but when we name these elements properly we see that they don't even exist! Thus astrology is largely based on imagined stories of imaginary gods. Is that something to believe in? Is that not a *false* religion?

To our big questions we need the balm of authentic answers, not myths. I am not imaginary. You are not fiction. Neither have we been created in the image of mythical non-gods. They did not give us our world; we gave them theirs! Being non-beings, the gods are ignorant even of themselves; so how much more unaware are they of us? What true and real answers can they supply?

If I were Jupiter, I suppose I would get along quite well by listening to the squawk of my mythical family. As a non-being, I could live consistent with myths, trusting in my family's mandates. Placing my non-life in submission to their non-existence would cause me no harm. My nothingness would be consistent with theirs; myths would be true to who and what I was. In the imaginary world of non-being, non-answers and non-sense would be just fine. But I am neither Jupiter nor myth. I am real. You are real. The external world is there, and all is not fine. Nor will things improve if our culture, or an individual, complies with myth.

Thus, even if the smokescreen of phony nomenclature suddenly were blown away by the introduction of honest terminology, even if the terminology were changed, the results of one's obedience to myths would not change. Astrology's adherents would still be following a false religion, placing themselves in the service of something unreal. That would lead to a cruel bondage.

Am I being too harsh on mythology? After all, where did this mythology come from? The ancients recognized, as we do, that powers exist in the universe over which man has little control—suprahuman powers. Human beings have imagination. One can easily understand the Greeks and Romans making up stories to account for the mystery, the nature, the identity, the causes of suprahuman powers felt in earthquakes, floods, volcanic eruptions, lightning, famine, or wind. These greater-than-human powers became their gods.

The powers of the sky became Zeus to the Greeks, later called Jupiter by the Romans. The powers of the waters became Poseidon, Neptune to the Romans. Ares (Mars) became responsible for wars; Hades (Pluto) for the realm of the dead. They all began to accrue to themselves thousands of myths throughout the years.

The stories can give us a lot to think about. And from them we can gain a broader picture of the mental climate in which they were thought up. We might even go so far as to say that some of them may have been born out of the search for authentic answers. But they aren't authentic; they're mythical.

Mythical principles do not have the substance or the nature of authentic answers. Authentic answers have nothing imaginary about them. Authentic answers must be *real,* eternally real. They must last. But the Roman myths died out on their own. They couldn't stand up to the subsequent scientific and philosophical scrutiny that humanity came up with. Truth, to be truth, must withstand the tests of time, must stand up to scrutiny, and Roman mythology fell short. Yet its remains are buried in the "scientific" structure of astrology.

So it cannot be rightly said of the gods that there is something lasting, or everlasting, about them. More properly, since they are non-beings, it could be said that there is something even less than *finite* about them. Why, even the gods' confinement in orbit demonstrates clearly and convincingly that they are helpless.

In summary, we find problems with the truthfulness of astrology. It claims to base its system on the attributes of the "planets," when it is really based on mythological "gods." Evasive and equivocal use of terms forces the distinction between "planet" and "god" to disappear. This misleading nomenclature indicates a lack of integrity. The imaginary-ness of the gods invalidates our trust in them. Non-existent gods do not provide authentic answers to the real, ultimate questions of life.

FIVE
MYTHOLOGICAL RELATIVISM

Let's take a step further inside astrology, where we will find some other surprising boxes to unpack. The god-categories are but eight knowledge mines out of which astrologers dig legendary principles. Many other categories of information contain their own well-defined and fundamental principles, just as the gods do. It can get quite complex, but here is a simple way to look at it.

Astrology is like a large cube made up of small cube-categories of information.

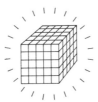

As the diagram shows, there is a world of categories: the sun-sign, the moon-sign, the ascendant, the eight planets (gods), the twelve signs of the Zodiac, the twelve houses of the horoscope, aspects, progressions, transits, retrogrades, the gods in each of the signs, the gods in each of the houses, and more. Every category encloses its own well-defined and fundamental principles. An astrology text could easily devote two or three hundred pages to defining what principles are unique to each category and how they interact.

The serious astrologer's task is immense. He performs something like mental gymnastics of an Olympian caliber. He must be trained to excerpt from each category the multitude of specific principles that correspond to the horoscope that he has before him. Yet pulling them out is not enough. He must also be trained to mix the excerpted principles. The excerpted principles are useless while standing alone. They need to be blended, or mixed, in accordance with astrological rules. Through this tedious process of first mining and then mixing ingredients, an astrologer derives in-depth astrological answers. Notice how this lengthy and involved methodology differs from the simplistic charlatan forms of astrology, such as newspaper horoscopes and starscrolls.

There would be no religion-science of astrology if the principles remained either holed up in the cube or excerpted to stand alone. There would be no in-depth answers. Astrology would be boring. We would quickly tire of it, for it would have so little to say. It would be next to useless. If the imposing government buildings in Washington, D.C., stood there full of laws yet lacked the interaction necessary to make them work—to govern the people—then Washington would have no say in our lives. It would be unable to govern, and therefore be useless to the people. Astrology is useful because astrologers are trained to mix the principles so as to fabricate a seemingly infinite number of answers, which in turn gives astrology quite a mouth. By this many lives are governed. This is the sense in which the religion-science exercises control.

Astrology has in-depth answers only because of the blending of principles from one category with those of another. For example, those of the gods are blended with those of the signs and with those of the houses. What is important is that we discover the *natures* of these interacting principles. If we can discover that, we will have also discovered the nature of serious astrological answers.

We have previously noted that the nature of the planetary influences is mythological. This is also true of the *signs*. Here is a glimpse at another major pillar. It is made up of the twelve categories of the astrological signs of the Zodiac. The sign Taurus represents a bull, and "was placed among the stars to commemorate the form that Zeus took when he carried Europa off to Crete. . . ."

Typhon, or Typhoeus, was a horrible creature that had "a hundred burning snake heads and spoke with the voices of men and animals." This hideous monster tried to overthrow the gods and rule the universe. It is said that Zeus fought the monster with lightning and finally crushed its smoking body with the mountain Aetna, flinging it into Tartarus where it became the source of all harmful winds. The two fish pictured in the sign Pisces are the goddess Aphrodite and her son Eros, who took the shape of fish and "leaped into the Euphrates River in order to escape the monster Typhon."

Hydra was another hideous, many-faced creature. "Half-sister of the Nemean lion through either its father, Typhon, or its mother, Echinda." Hydra lived near the spring, Amymone, at Lerna, "in company with its devoted friend, a large crab." Heracles (Hercules), out to kill Hydra, engaged in battle with the creature by hacking away at its heads with his sword. During the battle, Heracles was caught around his foot by one of Hydra's limbs. To make matters worse, Hydra's ally the crab "sallied from the swamp and began biting Heracles' foot." Heracles eventually destroyed Hydra, but the devoted crab, in faithful service to Hydra, was immortalized by the goddess Hera as the constellation Cancer.

The Archer, that personage represented in the sign Sagittarius, "is said to be Crotus, son of Pan, by Eupheme, the Muses' nurse. Crotus was a favorite of the Muses, who asked Zeus to immortalize him in the sky."[5]

On and on and on go these tales. As with the god categories, so with the signs. The signs of the Zodiac offer us the same perilous situation that exists in the god categories. Another major astrological pillar is filled with air. Yet, because of the *mixing* of the principles, the mischief doubles and triples, or more. You're not just getting one myth, you're getting a mixture of plenty. Let us say that your birth chart contains the god Jupiter in the sign Sagittarius in the second house. The imaginary principles of Jupiter, Sagittarius, and the second house must be blended. From this mixture you would have your in-depth astrological answer. But, again, the *nature* of the answer is the real hassle, especially when you attempt to build a life upon it. It is much worse than building upon sand—it's building upon air.

One may rightly argue that this religion-science is so much more than the myths of Venus in Libra, Uranus in Scorpio,

Saturn in Aries, or Mars in Leo. Yes, the illustration of Jupiter in Sagittarius is simplistic. The mixing of the principles is usually much more involved. Jupiter in Sagittarius is illustrated only to indicate the actual nature of a serious astrological answer, commonly called a delineation. And *the mythical nature never changes,* no matter how many principles are mixed.

A client's chart may indeed have Jupiter in Sagittarius. That Jupiter would stand alone, unaspected, is unlikely. Other gods could be in *aspect* to Jupiter.

Briefly, aspects of the planets are simple geometric relationships between the earth and two or more of the planets (gods) as they are located in the solar system during the time for which the horoscope was constructed. Squares and opposites are considered adverse or difficult aspects; trines and sextiles, favorable or helpful. Conjunctions could be favorable or adverse.

The client with Jupiter in Sagittarius could have Venus, or another planet, in relationship (aspect) to Jupiter. This being so, the myths of Venus, and its sign and house, would need to be blended with Jupiter's. (By now you have probably guessed that the houses also contain principles rooted in mythology.) All of the horoscope's mythical ingredients then, must be blended together to cast serious delineations. And no matter how complex the delineations, no matter how many ingredients modify the answers, their mythical nature never changes. They remain imaginary. There is a traffic jam of legends and myths everywhere.

Let's try to simplify this. A few insights into several principles contained in the cube categories of the houses, signs, and aspects will help you see how this mythological relativism works out in a typical astrological counseling session.

As noted, aspects are geometric relationships between the gods, having diverse meanings: adverse, favorable, neutral. Concerning the twelve signs, each is said to rule over a different part of the human body. Aries rules the head; Taurus, the throat and neck; Capricorn is said to govern the stomach. The twelve houses, simply numbered one through twelve, govern different departments of life. The second house controls one's finances and possessions; the fifth house principles involve children; the seventh, partners and unity with others, and so on. And concerning the gods, whenever one is located in its home (or ruling) sign, for example, Mars in Aries or Saturn in Capricorn, it is said to be exalted or dignified, meaning that the highest part of its nature will be brought out, as an influence. The gods, however, are always traveling in their orbits, meaning that every so often a god will spend some time occupying the sign of the Zodiac opposite to the one it rules, for example, Mars in Libra or Saturn in Cancer. Whenever this occurs, the god's nature is said to be debilitated, and the lowest part of its nature will be brought out. (I guess it's cranky from being away from home.)

We can now make some general delineations. In a client's chart, if Jupiter is unaspected in the second house (finances) and if that house happens to be Sagittarius (making Jupiter exalted), an astrologer should make a delineation something like, "The principles of expansion and good fortune (Jupiter) exalted in the second house will bring you much financial success without having to work too hard for it." A second person could have Saturn unaspected and debilitated in the sign Cancer in that house. The reading, then, would change to something like, "There will be a regular pattern of constricting or withholding of finances. You will need to work hard for financial stability."

In the first reading, principles of an exalted Jupiter mix with second-house myths in the sign Sagittarius. In the second, debilitated Saturnian principles interact in the same house but in Cancer. The astrologer mined myths out of the categories of the gods, the signs, the houses. Once excerpted, he blended them together in accordance with the guidelines set forth in the texts.

You walk away from that counseling session with some answers. This is how astrology begins to govern, to control. The governing can be even more complex. This is when the "aspects" come into the picture. A third person could have a horoscope similar to the second, but with an adverse aspect of Venus square to Saturn. The myths of Venus and whatever house and sign it is in must be factored into Saturn debilitated in Cancer in the second house. The delineation would adjust to something like, "You will probably be unsuccessful, financially, in acting, writing, music, and the arts." Furthermore, it is common for other gods to be in aspect to these aspects, and so on. It is quite an ordeal to figure out an entire horoscope. A mythological

relativism builds, and builds, and builds, giving horoscope reading definition, telling you what your horoscope is saying, and
allowing you, thereby, to let it govern your life.

And it *seems* real. It seems as if the elemental laws of the
universe are being interpreted for you. It seems as though you
are being given the keys to becoming happy and self-governing
and more independent. But the whole thing is jammed with
myths. We must come to grips with the fact that this mythological relativism has no *real* conversation or communication, no
real connection, no *real* relationships with reality. The complex
interrelationships, which seem to support the various principles, have no substance—they can support nothing, they offer
no help, they interpret nothing.

Yet, as was said, I am real. You are real. The external world is
there, and all is not fine. Nor will the issues in our lives improve
if we comply with myths. Compliance with myths straps us to a
merciless bondage that will inevitably destroy us by pushing us,
one day at a time, closer to the edge of the real universe—until
one day we are pushed out.[6] This is one of the demands the
system of astrology makes on us. This should make us shudder,
precisely at this point. For it is clear that a government rooted
in a mythological relativism cannot grant rights to liberty, but
instead deprives the human being of freedom and dignity. Its
rationale fools with our powers of judgment; its rule over us
paralyzes our initiative. It promises freedom but swipes the pre-
cious few freedoms that we do possess. Instead of releasing its
disciples, astrology subtly congeals the personality into a sub-
human likeness by slowly, daily, sifting out of our personalities
what is real, as we submit even more deeply to its rule.

If this is so obvious now, why have we not noticed it before?
Why is astrology a phenomenon that seems so real and solid, so
helpful? As we have seen, the first reason for this is the planetary nomenclature. But there are others. Try to visualize this
entire cube world as a block on the table in front of you. It
appears solid and real. Similar to jamming your knuckles
against an iron block, though certainly not as jarring, a real
feeling exists upon entering the astrological heavens. That real
feeling exists, secondly, because of its power, which we will discuss shortly. But it also exists, just as importantly, because astrology has a uniform structure, which can be viewed and

vaguely felt—like the cube world on the table. Many astrological principles are structured in a way that never changes; this gives the impression that they are real, something you can grab on to.

Even among diverse authors, astrology consists of certain maxims that never change. And people notice this. That is, Mars always rules Aries, Saturn always rules Capricorn. Leo is always a fire sign; it is never a water sign. Mercury represents Mercury, never another member of the family. Opposites and squares are always "difficult" aspects; trines and sextiles are always favorable. There are always three air signs, three earth signs, three water signs, and three fire signs. The second house always represents finances; the fourth house, family, and so on. So there is a certain uniform structure throughout astrology, but the maxims are imaginary! Just because they never change doesn't mean they are based on anything true. And unfortunately, real feelings are not necessarily the right road to truth. Someone has said that a line may be straight in only one way but crooked in a million or more.

Today we know something else about the iron block that hurts our fists. Billions of electrons scurry in a frenzy inside. The keen eyes of the scientists' instruments have discovered this. Similarly, the discerning eye of the light of truth discovers that the religion-science of astrology is something more (perhaps we should say less) than what it seems to be. Though the structural I-beams remain consistent, they are consistently mythical. On the table before us, we discover that astrology is not a real, solid world at all. It's more like a bubble. Attempt to grasp it, try to pick it up off the table, and it will burst apart, quickly to disintegrate, nothing more than a zero with the rim knocked off.

It is a long way to fall, from leaning against the imaginary pillars in the astrological heavens to the real earth below. Is anyone going to be able to fall such a distance without being crippled for life? The myths only entice, hoping to lure a person into an elaborate form of polytheism made up of a veritable hodgepodge of Greek and Roman non-gods and other mythical principles.

It is heartbreaking. We need to weep and pray for the uncountable number of well-intentioned, sensitive, and vulnerable persons who have fallen prey to the cube world of synthesized myths. They are caught in a mythical relativism whose trapdoor has silently snapped shut behind them, and are left alone to bump around in agony, unknowingly, against the sharp corners of many angles that will inevitably destroy them. What riches the myths may hope to bequeath, but what ruin they, in fact, will bequeath, is such a violent paradox that we ought to jump back with terror.

SIX
QUESTIONS FOR THE
ASTROLOGY-MINDED

As we have redefined astrology thus far, it has become exceedingly suspect. In fact, there's not much left to it except its power, which I will discuss in a later chapter. In this chapter I offer what may seem like just so much huffing and puffing, but these are significant marks against astrology that have never been sufficiently erased, any one of which could cast doubt on the veracity of the astrological system.

Please understand that this is not where a critique of astrology *starts*. It starts, as was stated, with the foundation: Astrology is based on mythology. But that very basic structural flaw shows itself in more surface details, which have been called into question over the years. I will not cover these arguments in detail, but I have included an appendix of book titles for study in these areas. Yet before I go on to talk about the power in astrology, here is a briefly stated list of some unresolvable and long-standing questions regarding the craft.

1. Above the Arctic Circle (66 degrees latitude) there may be no planet in sight for several weeks. And it is nearly impossible to calculate precisely what constellation or zodiacal point is rising on the horizon above that latitude. Why is this important? It means that some Greenlanders, northern Alaskans and Canadians, Siberians, and so on, have no horoscope. They have no planetary influence to determine their existence. Astrologically speaking, they were never born!

2. Until the 1500s, astrology was based on the assumption that the earth was the center of the solar system and that the planets revolved around it. Thus, before Copernicus, horoscopes were constructed upon that untrue knowledge about the solar system.

3. The outer planets of Uranus, Neptune, and Pluto were unseen, and thus unknown, to early astrologers. After each planet's discovery, it was then incorporated into astrological calculations and interpretations as an "influence." If these planets and their supposed influences were there all the time, yet not included in horoscope methodology, should not this oversight have invalidated previous horoscopes?

4. Identical twins born at the same time can grow up to lead dissimilar lives. In fact, one could die at birth and the other live to be eighty. If we extend first principles of astrological logic, without cheating, this should not be the case. The twins, growing up, should have the same "life-guidance" support system from the planets and the stars. One should not die at birth while the other lives on.[7]

5. The system of astrology says the "planets" of the solar system influence our lives from a great distance. And the bigger and closer the planet is to us, the greater its influence upon us. This is why the tiny speck of Pluto, so far away, is not reckoned by most astrologers to be a major "force" in one's life unless it is really prominent in the horoscope. Why, then, is there no mention of the influence of the planet closest to us? Why is the planet that is right under our feet ignored? Why are the natures of all the other gods and the sun and the moon tediously articulated, but there is no chart or list in which the earth's influence in human affairs is figured into astrological answers?

The earth should be a greater astrological factor, because of our closeness to it, than even the sun and the moon. Pages of information should be devoted to its part in the mythological equations of astrological answers. I have never seen an astrology book that does this. As a planet, doesn't the earth have an "influence"? Then maybe the others don't either. If the earth is left as an astrological blank in the solar system, except for the mathematical calculations of the astronomer, perhaps the other planets should be left blank as well.

6. Astrology says that the planets rule the signs of the Zodiac.

Yet the constellations, upon which the so-called Zodiac is over-laid, are light-years away from the planets. One wonders how anyone rules something that is so far distant.

7. Mass tragedies. If astrology imparts specific planetary influences to individual lives, then everyone should live *and* die in a different way. How can it be then, since all horoscopes are different, that thousands of people (of all ages and different walks of life) can die in a mass tragedy, or millions in a holocaust? The astrological reply to this is that "mundane astrology" (the branch of astrology dealing with nations and events) over-rules "natal astrology" (the type dealing with individual lives; we've been discussing natal astrology in this book). Yet this is an impossible answer. For the fact remains that natal astrology claims to determine, with a fair amount of certainty, the destiny of an individual, which results from the planetary influences the person supposedly inbreathed at birth and fleshed out in life, all the way to the end. The whole natal system is based on the principle that unique planetary forces determine each individual's destiny. Now either this is the teaching or it is not. Astrology says that it is.

Yet you cannot have it both ways. That is, if mundane astrology *overrules* natal astrology, this means that natal astrology operates in a way other than the books explain. In other words, mundane astrology does not simply overrule, it *invalidates* natal astrology, because it attacks its first principles. If this is so, natal astrology is no more. Either mass tragedies or mundane astrology invalidates natal astrology. Take your pick.

Now astrologers have set replies to such arguments. And I don't blame them. Their sanity is at stake. And I'll show you why. They have seen the system "work," and yet here are some convincing arguments (what's worse, usually from those who don't believe it can work) saying that it cannot. The astrologer reacts to this. His experience proves that it works; therefore he feels these arguments must be wrong. So he must build a case to refute each argument. The astrologer feels that if, say, point one cannot be refuted, then astrology should not work. But he cannot honestly admit that such might be the case; he has seen astrology work. So he is forced, by the silences of the practice, to manufacture a seemingly satisfactory reply to each question, almost in order to keep his sanity. For he cannot understand how the system can work apart from the way he has been taught. Since he believes that the books cannot be wrong, he feels the opposing arguments must be incorrect. And so he must out-argue the arguers.

But in all honesty, these refutations are imaginary, too. They are formulated by using the astrological rationale, which we have seen to be mythological. They, too, belong in the cube world with the rest of the mythological relativism. I know this is difficult to accept. It was difficult—no, it was *impossible*—for me to accept this when I was a believer in astrology. I can tell you I had all the necessary refutations packed away as ammunition ready to fire. And times came when I had to fire these bullets. But in all honesty, they shoot down nothing. Oh, they sounded great. But it would have been far better for me, at the time, to take this medicine, gulp down the fact that the texts are deceptive, accept the difficult truth that this system must work in a way completely different from what the texts describe, and *then* go on, if I still wanted to, and discover what its power really is. This we shall now do.

SEVEN
SELF-DISCLOSURE

Now we come face to face with the most telling argument in favor of astrology: It works. Despite everything else that is fictitious about it, it nevertheless reveals things about people that couldn't be known unless there were power in it. I call these phenomena *self-disclosures*.

Astrology demands commitment from its spokespersons, the astrologers. As they become more seasoned at the craft, astrologers are enabled to discover, from someone's horoscope, details or particulars surrounding the person's life. These special discoveries are self-disclosures. To help us better understand their nature, let's look first at two categories of information that are *not* self-disclosures.

First, *speculations* are not self-disclosures. Speculations are guesses about one's life using plenty of abstract or ambiguous language from only the sun-signs, or the moon-signs, or the ascendant. Speculations are easy to spot. Newspaper "horoscopes," sun-sign and moon-sign paperbacks, and those little scrolls are the most common. Using only a person's sun-sign, moon-sign, or ascendant, astrologers make vague and open-ended guesses, using ambiguous terms about why people are the way they are, or what they should or should not be doing, or what may or may not be currently happening to them.

One could look anywhere; these appeared in the July 8, 1983, *Detroit Free Press.* "Scorpio: creative endeavors get a boost from a distant source. Capricorn: future success depends on sacrifices made now. Aries: you have nothing to lose by making a request. Gemini: keep your integrity no matter what the social pressure." In another place, one speculation simply blared, "Expect triumph!" Notice the ambiguous language. There are no specific disclosures. Though they do carry a bit of advice and encouragement that we would all like to hear now and then, remember that the advice has its roots in mythology. And since they are loaded with ambiguous language, speculations are open-ended, subject to numerous interpretations. How far off is the distant source of the Scorpio person, 25 or 2500 miles, or neither? And what is the boost? If Aunt Sally in Boston sends me a check in Albuquerque for the Indian quilt I knitted, or if my apple-rhubarb pie wins first prize at the state fair, which is the fulfillment? Or is it none of these and I must wait for another? And, what about the speculation that shouted, "Expect triumph!" At what? A math test, a bowling championship, the Olympics? Speculations leave it up to you to decide.

Second, *generalizations* are not self-disclosures, though they are closer to them. Generalization is a synonym for the mythological relativism discussed previously. Astrologers apply most of their time and energy to generalizations. To acquire the skills of delineating the myths, beginning astrologers need to collect many charts. They usually collect charts of friends, relatives, and the immediate family, for these are the easiest to get. After a time, the student, with ten or twenty horoscopes to practice on, becomes knowledgeable in general astrological answers (delineations), which are derived from the mixed myths. As we saw previously, these delineations are limited to *general* statements regarding personality, relationships, employment, and so on. Generalizations, unlike speculations, are more in-depth. They are developed by using the entire religion-science. Generalizations, however, are not self-disclosures. And they, too, leave it up to you to decide what they mean, how to interpret them.

Though composed of mythology, speculations and generalizations have subsidized the mass interest in astrology because their composition makes catchy use of abstract language, which I'll discuss a bit more in a later chapter. It is *self-disclosures,* however, that champion the rise. Just as a gifted psychologist, therapist, or M.D. becomes well-known for being able to root out personal problems, so, too, astrology is popular because seasoned astrologers may track down, in one's horoscope, an actual character trait or specific past event. Or, they may disclose a current predicament, or advantage, that you face. And the word spreads. You, the client, leave fascinated, tell a friend, and so on.

Consider how unlikely this occurrence should be. It should not happen at all. As far as we know so far, astrology is a mythological relativism, and there's no way such relativism can produce accurate self-disclosures. That is, mythological relativism cannot know anything about anything. It has absolutely, and I mean *absolutely,* no way of knowing about real events. According to the intelligence report on astrology so far, self-disclosures are impossible.

A seasoned astrologer, however, knows better. He will tell you that self-disclosures do occur. Experienced numerologists or fortune-tellers will concur regarding their crafts; their clients will tell you the same. In this way, a large amount of trust develops on the part of the client, trust in the craft and in the spokesperson, as a few quarters of the client's life are laid open and recognized by someone who knows only the client's time, place, and date of birth.

So it is that self-disclosures become large dividends, justifying one's continued investment in the craft. Plus, the greater the precision and regularity of the dividends, the more excited one becomes about investing. Thus the phenomenon of self-disclosures helps to explain why many clients are unafraid to venture the next astrological step: trusting the craft to govern their futures. Self-disclosures, therefore, not only generate public trust in the system but also in the *forecasts* the system provides.

I cannot remember anyone who became less interested in astrology when it touched upon, not generalities, but obvious personal facts. I remember that night at Phyllis's house. Her boyfriend was there, and the three of us sat around her dining room table while I delineated her chart. (We were there a few hours.) I knew little about Phyllis. After discussing some generalizations with her, I began to "notice" (in a progression of her birth chart) that she currently faced severe adversity on her job, and that this ordeal was being perpetrated by a fellow employee.

Perhaps a supervisor, I thought. When I could not shake off this impression that was coming to me as I was looking over her chart, I spoke to Phyllis about it, suddenly adding that the ordeal had begun about a year and a half earlier. Phyllis confirmed my discovery.

There was also a curious slant to this delineation. When Phyllis confirmed the self-disclosure, I, for some reason, forecasted that within one year the ordeal would end. I did not know it, but this forecast fit Phyllis's desire. For years she had enjoyed her job, right up until the time that the conflict with this supervisor had begun. Finally, after almost two years, enough was enough. The strength and length of the conflict was wearing her down. She was thinking about resigning, even though she did not want to. Yet this night, Phyllis heard a forecast that suited her desire. Then Phyllis, motivated by the accuracy of the self-disclosure, let the forecast overthrow her thoughts about quitting. In other words, "I'll stick it out. I love my job and within a year I'll be able to enjoy it again." In this way astrology could begin to govern Phyllis.

I also remember Tom. Tom taught occult mind development classes. During one weekend seminar, he excited his students with an extraordinary account of how he had recently traveled many miles through astral projection. After hearing this story, I wanted to do his horoscope. I wanted to know the astrological *whys* of Tom's supposed powers of astral projection. Eventually, I erected Tom's chart and we discussed it. What sticks out in my mind about this discussion is Tom saying he was uninterested in astrology *before* I delineated his chart.

In fairness, I must point out that Tom's event was known to me before I did his chart and it was more subjective (on Tom's part) and less verifiable than something as real as Phyllis's ordeal. But I knew Tom. I doubt that he lied about the experience itself (whatever psychic thing it is that happens to trigger what is called astral travel). And he did have a witness. And it would be childish to say that it cannot occur. In the occult, incidents are bizarre and injudicious most of the time. The point is that in Tom's chart I saw strong indicators (influences) specifically for the supposed capability of astral travel as opposed to other forms of psychic manifestations. And I told him so. The self-disclosure for astral travel as being *currently* operative in Tom's life fit well, without cheating. Thus, though the horoscope did not disclose an unknown reality in his life, it nevertheless confirmed one. If I had not known about Tom's "powers," I saw such strong influences for them that I would have spoken to him about them anyway.

These two examples illustrate how self-disclosures differ from generalizations. Self-disclosures deal with the details, or particulars, of one's life. For Phyllis: a year and a half earlier a conflict began with her supervisor at work. For Tom: astral travel was currently and strongly operating. And for the girl I mentioned earlier: "small-boned." Thus, self-disclosures do not leave it up to you to decide what they mean and how to interpret them. Unlike speculations and generalizations, they tell you precisely what they mean. They are detailed and specific. They use concrete rather than abstract language, and thus they are not left open to various interpretations.

For the astrologer, a confirmation of a self-disclosure is an impressive moment. It is as though he had been attempting the impossible, say, to walk on water, when suddenly—a confirmation! Of course, confirmations also affect the clients. Besides getting them more interested in astrology, confirmations satisfy, at least temporarily, the thirst for an explanation to whatever is occurring in one's life. Through such confirmations, astrology promises answers to the big questions: Who am I? Why am I here? What's going on with me? Where am I going? We all sigh over these mysteries and long for "a tender word, to come and tell us who we are." If astrology can know one unknown thing about me, people think, perhaps it knows other things—things I don't even know about myself. Perhaps it *can* interpret human nature, and spiritual things as well. And thus, through astrological confirmations, the convinced clients transform a hobby into a way of life.

How can it happen? What gives astrologers that subtle personal knowledge about clients? It can't be the mythology. But what is it? These are thundering questions. And most of the public sleeps through them. For most adherents of astrology, it is enough that it "works." There is a fascination with the power, without a suspicion as to the nature of that power. "Why shouldn't I believe in it? What it said about me was right!" The line of reasoning goes something like this: The correct self-disclosures are not incorrect, therefore they must not be "wrong." Since they are not wrong, it must be all right to use astrology. But is this line of reasoning always right?

We need to be a bit analytical here. Though astrology works, it may not be OK to use it. Perhaps this religion-science leads to catastrophe. Is it wise to assume without question that the power in astrology is after our well-being? Someone has said that humility of mind produces a teachable spirit. Many experiences come to us in life, some being rather ugly, though we first see them dressed in happy garb. Even terrorists follow and use correct bomb-making disclosures, but no sane person is therefore convinced that it is right to make terrorism a way of life. That's an extreme example, to be sure. But we have been lulled to sleep. No one wants to think of what is in back of astrological self-disclosures. Things that we are asleep to, however, are sometimes the most important.

EIGHT
THE POWER BEHIND IT

So where do self-disclosures come from? We have various options, but some of them dissolve under close scrutiny. We have already seen that the official line of astrology—that knowledge is embedded in the planets and stars and their movement in the sky—is invalid, because the whole system is based on arbitrary assumptions drawn from ancient mythology.

Perhaps it's all a hoax: Astrologers hire private detectives to ferret out details of their client's lives. Maybe in a few rare cases this might be so, but I can say from personal experience that the self-disclosures I gave Phyllis and others were no hoax.

With natural means of knowledge ruled out, we must consider supernatural means. Many people get fidgety, however, when the discussion turns to this. For most, it's not really their fault. It is difficult for many these days to acknowledge the presence of a supernatural world. Materialism and, until recently, science and psychology have conditioned the modern West to believe that what is unseen does not exist. We have been bludgeoned by empiricism into paying attention only to what we touch and taste and see. But here we have no other choice. There is nowhere else to turn the discussion.

Self-disclosures come from some source beyond the astrologer and not from the rationale he claims. So we're left with more options: God, or the devil, may be the source and power—if we choose the Christian framework—or perhaps some demigod, powerful, but not all-powerful—if we choose another framework.

What *do* we know about the thing that causes astrological self-disclosures? It lies. Whatever it is, it wants astrologers and their clients to think the knowledge comes from the planets, when this is clearly not the case. Hence, the being is deceptive. This rules out the God of the Bible as the source, since God is true, in fact, the essence of Truth.

While the Bible records various "self-disclosures" given to men by God, it is always forthright about the source. It never plants deception. On the other hand, though God cannot be the power behind astrological self-disclosures, the Bible does record some incidents that fit this discussion of astrology in some fascinating ways. You should not get uneasy about reviewing these stories, since they remarkably illustrate, as no other document does, who or what we're after. It is sort of like seeing the face of the person you pass by in the shopping mall and noticing that it clearly resembles the face on the wanted poster you saw hanging in the post office yesterday. Never in a million years did you ever think you'd actually see a wanted criminal in person. But there he was. And you just cannot shake the resemblance. I think you will find something similar occurs when you look into the following records.

Just three chapters into the Bible there emerges a deceptive being aptly called the "serpent." Genesis 3:1-6 gives a description of his character and a look at his motive. It tells us he communicates to a woman named Eve in order to see her misled and mortally wounded. In this short yet highly concentrated narrative[8] we are given material to meditate upon for days. We discover that the serpent is a rebel in the universe, an enemy of God. He lies, he has verifiable information about three realities—God, the creation, and individual persons—and he uses this information in an all-out effort to ruin Eve and her husband.

The serpent begins his scheme by conversing with Eve. And *what* is his craft? The serpent gets Eve's ear through the presentation of self-disclosures! It seems he uses these for three reasons: to get her attention, to hold it, and to get her to tell someone else about them.

After Eve realizes the serpent is fairly accurate, she goes another step. She begins to reason with him, rationalizing away what she knows to be true, that is, what God has said to her and her husband. Then she goes yet another step, accepting his proposal and acting on it. But the serpent is a weasel. His advice—a promise to transform Eve into a more highly evolved being—is a lie. His counsel cheats her. It brings about her death. The serpent offers a personal revelation or two, but the record shows that the serpent's aim is to bring suffering to those who listen to him—in this case, the suffering of death. This is definitely an evil power, not a neutral force. Thus, from these six short verses in Genesis, we have a description that fits the being we are after. We also get a look at his motives and some insights into hidden aspects of his system of communication.

Notice again how the deception began. The serpent is not stupid. He is clever enough to know that Eve will not stay tuned, nor will she follow his advice or tell it to others if he babbles nonsense that contradicts the facts as Eve knows them. Nor will she listen if he comes across as ill-willed. (Think back to the incident with Phyllis and recall how perfectly this matches.) Therefore, to seem credible, the serpent mentions a few things that correspond to what Eve knows to be true about herself. To seem benevolent, he guides the conversation in a matter that will make Eve think he is kind and that he is concerned about her well-being and future, her evolution. Unfortunately, it seems as though Eve did not notice the serpent's hidden agenda to destroy, though she did have the clear message from God not to fool with it. We, on this side of her history, can see clearly that the serpent's motive was evil. Viciousness was behind his self-disclosures. He wanted to see Eve in the morgue. And it all began with self-disclosures.

The serpent tricked Eve, through the self-disclosures, into disregarding what God had said. God knew that Eve and her husband would die if they ate the fruit of a certain tree in the Garden of Eden.[9] And God, in his compassion and care for them, wanted to protect them from dying without taking away their free wills and turning them into machines. So he simply told them not to eat anything from that tree, and he told them what would happen to them if they did. The serpent's innuendoes, however, quickly undermine what God had said. And

Eve's faith in God's tenets soon eroded. Believing the serpent's voice, she not only obeyed him herself but she was influenced and then transformed enough to communicate the serpentine enlightenment to Adam, her husband; then he, too, obeyed the death counsel. The self-disclosures implied that they were about to partake of a life-style that would assist them in a spiritual evolution. Both were talked into believing this. Yet immediately what God had said, not what the serpent had promised, came true. Adam and his wife began to suffer. They did not evolve. They died. As God had said.

Notice again what this story shows us. Accurate self-disclosures generated trust. That trust led to deception. That deception brought about bad actions. The bad actions resulted in destruction.

In the biblical Book of Job we get a longer glimpse, from a different angle, into hidden aspects of the deceptive supernatural world. As the curtain is drawn back further, in the first two chapters of Job, the scenes vibrate with drama.[10]

In Job, the deceptive being is given the name Satan, "false accuser." And here he seems as resolutely inflamed against humanity as he was in the Garden of Eden. This time we get to see him a bit less disguised, clearly mad with destroying. His tactics differ, but his motive is the same. Here, to cause ruin and death, Satan, as a hellish prosecuting attorney, foams a diatribe against the man Job in the courtroom of God. The scene shifts from the Garden to the courtroom because Satan has a real problem with Job. He wants to lead Job into destruction, but Job will not be a part of any system of communication with the evil supernatural world. Job's ear is tuned to God alone. He will not listen to self-disclosures from deceptive beings. And Satan knows that he will not be able to get Job's ear. "Therefore," perhaps he says to himself, "one day I'll get Job's attention."

Satan knew Job remarkably well. He knew that Job was one of the mightiest men of his time, sort of like a modern-day billionaire. He knew Job's family, his sons, his daughters, his wife. He knew who the hundreds of Job's servants were. He knew all about Job's wealth and vast possessions. He knew that Job was loyal to God and feared him. Details. Particulars. Facts. All this Satan knew about this individual. And Satan figures (mistakenly, we see later) that Job obeys God only because God has given him so much. But he cannot get Job's ear to lead him astray. And he still wants to see Job destroyed. So, appearing before God one day, he connives the bait of a false accusation against Job. Satan rallies his devilish psychology and counsel before God, charging that Job will curse God to his face if everything is taken away from him.[11]

But this accusation proves to be false. Job remains true to God, even after Satan slays Job's servants, burns his sheep and cattle, murders his sons and daughters, and strikes Job with cancers from head to foot! Job is close to death for months, not even knowing why. For he does not have the record to read, as we do. He does not know what is going on behind the "seens." Yet even in such disgusting condition—in anguish, in pain, with miserable company, with no relief, filled with doubts, moaning over the craziness of it all—Job remains faithful to God. Satan can only destroy him to a point, though he was hoping to take his life eventually. (Note that after Job's grievous losses, God gives him twice as much as he previously had.)

From the record here, not only is it affirmed that this deceptive being is a knowledgeable communicator out to destroy, but also that he converses with God as well as with humans. We also learn that he is mobile, roaming the earth, paying close attention to how humans think and reason. Furthermore, the record reveals a mighty truth: Satan is not an equal opposite God; he is answerable to God, under God's rule.

The accounts in Genesis and Job make it absolutely clear that this deceptive being is a murderer, out to destroy human life, not to mention anything else in the vicinity that has meaning to its owners, and that he will use self-disclosures for this purpose if he needs to. Many other narratives warn the reader about this horrid being, who is given different names according to the treacherous aspects of his character. He is not afraid of bizarre evil, either. This is seen in his temptations of Jesus. Here he is given the name "the devil." While Jesus is fasting in the wilderness of Galilee, what does the devil tempt him to do? To kill himself.[12] It is the same scenario—the ingeniously laid stratagem of self-disclosures—yet with a slightly different tactic. The devil hopes to use self-disclosures about Jesus from the Old Testament to deceive him.

With Jesus, the devil has a similar problem to the one he had with Job. Jesus will not obey any system of communication within the world of this deceptive being. Jesus only listens to his Father. Yet, knowing that the Old Testament often speaks of Jesus, and knowing that Jesus has an excellent knowledge of this, the devil masterminds a plan of Scripture twisting,[13] hoping to catch Jesus off guard and draw him into obeying a lie. If he can get Jesus to believe twisted self-disclosures and interpretations about himself, then Jesus may fall. Obedience to his Father will have been replaced by obedience to counsel from the supernatural world of deception. This is how the serpent caused the ruin of Adam and Eve. It is how Satan was hoping to have Job killed. But Jesus is the Word.[14] He is the truth.[15] Therefore he is highly sensitive to error and Scripture twisting. He cannot be fooled. He will not be led into obeying a lie. With correct interpretation of the Scriptures, Jesus rightly applies the knowledge there and commands the devil to leave his presence. This selection from Matthew's Gospel records that this deceptive being not only knows about God, mankind, and creation—he knows the Bible, too, and how to distort its meaning.

Contrary to much modern thought, the Bible clearly supports the existence of a deceptive, spiritual world of evil that, though unseen, is no less real than the world we do see.

It adds that the devil is the ruler of this unseen world of deception and commands a mob of deceiving beings like himself.[16] Working together under the devil's leadership, in their rebellion against God and their hatred of humanity,[17] these spirit beings work undercover, through what have become known as occult systems of communication, to deceive, to lead astray, to destroy. I realize this is not a pleasant truth. I don't think most people have much of a clue at first as to what they are getting involved with in the occult. For the thing about deception *is* its deception. It involves deliberate concealment or misrepresentation of truth by the deceiver, so that the one being lied to will not realize the intent of the deceiver to lead her into error or danger.

These deceptive systems of communication within the unseen realm of the universe are called "occult"—hidden—because from them you can get otherwise hidden information. The thing wrong with occult hidden data is the vile motive attached to it; the occult wants to see its adherents suffer—not

right away necessarily, but in the end. The communication between the serpent and Eve is a perfect sample of occult disclosures emanating from deceptive beings whose sole motive is the
slow suicide of the individual, while pretending to help that
person evolve spiritually. We don't know which of these practices was the first or the most popular. Such information is lost
with the ancients. The biblical record, however, does mention
some of the older and more popular ones: spiritualism, witchcraft (black or white), magic (black or white), sorcery, divination (any kind of fortune-telling) and, yes, astrology.[18]

The biblical record is not trying to be harsh by declaring
these systems off limits.[19] This has often been misunderstood. It
speaks as it does, not to shut us off from intellectual pursuits
and gaining genuine wisdom, but to warn us of the deception
from spiritual guides in that supernatural realm, that we may be
spared from the inevitable maltreatment of the deception. No
one would ever know that that world was a realm of deception if
the Bible didn't tell us. The occult will never tell its disciples
that.

Do we really want to be spared the domination and cruelty of
deception? Whatever the occult is, it is not good for us. This is
another place where we have been misled. In so many words, we
are told by its methodologies that they will enlighten us, push
us further up the evolutionary ladder, and transform us into
gods, that we may live forever in blissful union with some divine
Something somewhere. Yet the truth is that occult teaching is
the product of deceitful beings who want to see you ruined
eternally.[20] And God in his care for us has written to tell us.

But if you are not a Christian, even the stern warnings of the
Bible may not be enough for you. Yet, at the very least, you must
be impressed with how the biblical stories fit the situation at
hand. The questions we are asking in this book (What is the
source of self-disclosures? What do we know about the natures
of this source? How do the self-disclosures come?) are answered
in a remarkable, workable way by these ancient stories, though
these answers may be difficult for us to accept.

We are police detectives, in a way, seeking who is responsible
for these self-disclosures. Through study and logic we have
compiled his *modus operandi.* And suddenly, from some ancient files, comes a dossier on this character—the devil, the

serpent, Satan—who is wanted for similar activities. He fits the description perfectly, like no other during the investigation. Even if you reserve some doubts about those eyewitness reports from the files, the match should be close enough for you to make him your prime suspect.

And if you still find it difficult to buy all this "devil" business, you still have your *modus operandi,* your composite sketch. You still have to trace back these self-disclosures to some supernatural being that has knowledge but uses it to deceive. The question is begged: Is this the kind of guy you want to hang around with? As you continue your search through life for the authentic answers to the big questions, is this character going to help you or hurt you? He is likely to tease you with huge promises that he won't deliver.

NINE
HOW IT WORKS

By eliminating all the other "suspects" during our investigation, we are building a case for the conviction that this deceptive being, the devil, and the mob he rules lie behind the astrological self-disclosures. Because our age largely disbelieves in the unseen evil supernatural world, it has come up with a naturalistic and "scientific" explanation as to why astrology works. But as we look honestly at astrology, we begin to see that adherents of this system—without knowing it—are banging on the door through which communication is established with knowledgeable yet deceptive spirit beings. Eventually that door opens. And that opening produces an appalling development in the adherent's life. He or she matures in the craft in a most unthought-of manner: as a spirit medium.

Without contact with spirit beings, there would be no astrological self-disclosures. Or if they did come, it would be almost entirely from guesswork; they would be very rare. There would be no self-disclosures to "confirm" astrology apart from the intelligence imparted by these spirit beings to their spokespersons, the astrologers.

Today it is trendy to call these deceitful spirit beings evolved masters, adepts, alchemists, Universal Mind, telepathy, ESP, clairvoyance, mind development, spiritual guides, the Force, and so on. But such pseudonyms hide the real essence of these beings. So today we encounter the same deception that was faced by the ancients who tapped these resources. People today do not have the slightest idea that they are being asked to walk into a world of dangerous, deceptive beings.

I was never taught (most astrology students would say the same) that such spirit beings are in back of the self-disclosures. Astrological literature is silent regarding these informants, because it has its own defense for what is behind the self-disclosures. As we have seen, the texts teach that at birth each individual inbreathes his or her own particular "planetary" influences, which are dependent upon time, place, and date of birth. Therefore, if an astrologer delineates a self-disclosure, it is supposedly due to his cleverness at discerning or interpreting the specific influences inbreathed at birth as they relate to today. We have, however, dug beneath the surface of this proposition, discovering that there is no such thing as an astrological planetary influence. Indeed, there is gravity; and other "influences" in the solar system, such as magnetism, have been identified by astronomers and scientists. But astrology is not astronomy. Astrology is not concerned with planetary influences. It is concerned with mythological stories and deceitful supernatural influences. Its texts should divulge that at birth we inbreathe myths and that for self-disclosures we give ear to deceitful spirit beings. How different our understanding of astrology would be with that truth and candor appearing in the texts! How different our picture of the astrological heavens would be! Few people would want to travel *there*.

We need to stop ignoring the dangers of astrology and realize how they may affect our lives. But even in the world of the occult, evil spirits are not a popular subject these days. As has been mentioned, our scientific and mechanistic age comes equipped with a certain mischief: loss of the knowledge of the supernatural. This disbelief in anything supernatural has carried over into the literature of the occult, including astrology. A theory of disbelief in the supernatural floats in bits and pieces inside the head of the modern astrologer. Subsequently, this theory works itself out in his writings. Modern astrology (since the 1890s), therefore, usually excludes the supernatural as the reason for the self-disclosures and writes in a scientific and naturalistic dogma, that of "planetary influences." Thus, a modernized person will accept the astrological answer as to why it "works" but reject the real reason as a horrible Puritan superstition.

We need to realize that disbelieving in the supernatural is a new development connected with the modern Western world, associated only with the last hundred years or so. We are the odd civilization out, not previous civilizations. Thousands of years of recorded history tell us that this is so. We would have been considered backward and mixed up if we lived in the past disbelieving in the supernatural. And even today many third-world countries may consider us strangely ignorant of the spiritual realm. Past ages widely substantiated the existence of the evil supernatural world. It was a given. It was there. And they knew it. Were they all lying? If not, where did it go? It is a poor detective who will dismiss as out-of-date thousands of years of recorded testimony that gives evidence of the unseen world. You may edit it out of your textbooks or change its name, but you will not rub it out of existence.

Yes, there are occultists who affirm the presence of the supernatural. But even these occult mind-sets have been modernized. They would not agree that these spirit beings are deceptive and ill-willed toward humanity and that we should distance ourselves from them. Perhaps this is a clue as to why the occultist, who in some measure believes in the unseen, prefers that these malevolent entities be given the likable pen names of evolved masters, spiritual guides, the Force, etc. For such names hint that the supernatural, which interests occultists to varying degrees, exists, yet they remove every connotation of evil. Friendship is manufactured. Perhaps these shifty creatures use these trendy new names to promote an attractiveness to people in a modern West that disbelieves in supernatural evil. Their biblical names, however, help us see through the facades into their actual natures. Their rightful names are consistent with their horrid characters. They are rightly known as fallen angels, demons, and devils. They are called "foul," "lying," "unclean," "evil," and "deceiving." These frightful descriptions provide a clear understanding of what we're dealing with, if we'd stop overlooking it.

At this point you might ask, "Why isn't the astrologer aware? How can this communication with spirit beings occur if he doesn't even realize it?"

Though it is not possible to answer this question thoroughly, we can be sure of one thing. The nexus between this world and that world takes place where we do our thinking, in our invisible minds, where we understand things. Through a slick hook-up between worlds, details are somehow incorporated into the mind, our understanding keys in on them, and we begin conversing in our minds with them.

Yet this hook-up between spirit and spokesperson is subtle. It is not like a phone connection. It is not obvious that information is trickling in from the outside. The certainty of recognizing that there is a voice on the other end is strangely unapparent. The knowledgeable, familiar spirit infiltrates the thinking activity in such a covert way that the astrologer assimilates the data and has no inkling that anything other than his own thought life is responsible for the self-disclosures.

I cannot say how this cover-up works, but it is possible to discover *when* it occurs. If you have been an astrologer, consider the following occurrence. (If you have been involved in any occult craft, the following principle can be applied also. Simply substitute the terms appropriate to your system, say, tarot or palmistry, for the words *astrology* or *horoscope.*) You have a new horoscope before you. You begin to notice that a certain item in the chart gets your attention. It sticks out in your mind, softly glaring at you. You then begin to dwell upon its meaning. Perhaps a particular aspect of the chart pops into view, one you had not noticed before. It becomes difficult to shake off this impression that you "see" in the chart. After some consideration, you feel that this has relevance for your client. So you begin to discuss it with him or her.

What is occurring? The spokesperson's mind is becoming focused upon a portion of the chart that pertains to a detail in a client's life. This is a detail that a familiar spirit is privy to. It is the spirit that is somehow doing the "focusing." The focusing is influenced not by a planet or a mythological relativism but by a deceptive invisible being who knows both the spokesperson and the client. The spirit is like the top point of a triangle, seeing down to both astrologer and client.

I was not aware of the defiance Phyllis faced at work. I had no idea that Tom's horoscope would indicate clear and strong "influences" for astral travel. But the spirits knew these details.

And because I was the spokesperson, having had the astrological training necessary to recognize the particular mythological relatives that would indicate these specific hot-spots in the client's life, while I was studying the charts the spirits made the psychic connection and tied it all together.

In much the same way that the palm of the hand or the crystal is "contact material" for the fortune-teller, the horoscopic *chart* is used by the astrologer. It is the mediumistic point of interaction. Get rid of the contact material with the visible world and the spirits have no point of contact to make the psychic connection, to seep information through the spokesperson to the client.

Furthermore, because the spirits are both knowledgeable *and* mobile, it does not matter where the readings take place or with whom—as is also true with palm, tarot, and crystal ball readers. What matters is that "contact material" (horoscope) and a medium are present. The spirits will show. Self-disclosures will come.

Many have a hard time believing that these spirits are so completely and inexorably evil, *always* after humanity's ruin. Probably because we live with our *human* nature, we find it difficult to think that these spirits do not have a "nice" side to them, as modern occult teaching says they do. This is to say that no matter how depraved a human becomes, we know that that person may still have a good side. This potential, however, does not apply to evil spirits.

The partnership between spirit and spokesperson harms the latter tremendously. This is not just because the spokesperson becomes a medium for deception but because mediumship, which in some circles is now being called "transformation," is the foreplay of a deeper intercourse with these spirits: possession. Yet no matter what the degree of involvement, intimacy with the deceptive beings brings about the deterioration of anyone who remains in counsel with them, though he may not realize it. These spirits will draw him down into their totally depraved state. He will not be able to lift them to his "goodness." They cannot pull him up into a spiritual evolution, only down into their mess.

I do not enjoy writing this. I know that many have given their undivided loyalty, in sincerity, to the occult rationale, as I had, believing they are getting in tune with helpful spiritual guides and so on, believing they are being raised to higher spiritual planes. What I now know about these practices I wish I had discovered before I entered camaraderie with them, though I thank God that he has helped me out. And I pass these things on to you because I care. I am not out to deceive you. Major sorrows came my way due to my involvement with astrology. I did not understand that I would have been spared some major life disasters if I had not listened to the occult. Thus I am burdened for those in such a life-style, hoping they may be spared the maltreatment of deception.

I think it was C. S. Lewis who said that evil is fissiparous. The impending outcome of a medium's continued intercourse with the unseen world of evil spirits is his or her disintegration into the awful likeness of these beings, whose natures are evil and cannot be changed. With some persons, the breakdown is inch by inch, taking twenty or thirty years. Others may find themselves under psychiatric care after only a few years. Many adherents find they are suicidal or battling fear continually. The deterioration may vary in degree and in passage of time, yet the final results are the same. The union of an evil spirit with a human person will one day give birth to a madness that will destroy the human. Unless a medium forsakes the occult life-style, he will decay physically, psychologically, mentally, and spiritually, becoming more and more like the insane reality that communicates with him. Only time separates the medium from this end.

TEN
ABSTRACT LANGUAGE

A friend of mine, I'll call her Elaine, told me about a conversation she once had with someone we'll call Ed. Elaine had mentioned that she was interested in the arts, and Ed guessed that she must have "a lot of Venus" in her horoscope. Now Ed did not know much about astrology, but he had read a bit about it and retained some of the information. And as it turned out, he was right. Elaine had done her horoscope and remembered that Venus did in fact hold a prominent place there. Both of them left that conversation with a higher opinion of astrology. The incident had confirmed the "accuracy" of the astrological system in their minds. It seemed to work.

What's going on here? This is a very common occurrence. Many people find that astrology makes fascinating small-talk. And often, though not always, the conversations seem to confirm astrology's reliability and boost its public image.

Elaine and Ed and the countless others who experience this have no desire to be spirit mediums. They are not even very deeply into astrology. It is a hobby, a game, a conversation piece. But they are still playing with fire. Whether they know it or not, deceptive spirits are using the ambiguities of astrology's abstract language to draw people further into the craft.

The main deception here concerns *accuracy*. Earlier I mentioned that people may find speculations (such as the daily horoscope column in the paper) or generalizations ("Venus makes people artsy") to be "accurate," on occasion. If, as we have found, the major pillar of astrology (planetary influence) is invalid, how can this be? A closer look at this phenomenon, along with a tighter definition of accuracy, will help us understand.

If you took a class on communications, you would be taught that for *accuracy* you would need to use concrete rather than abstract language. For instance, a good radio broadcaster is taught to use concrete words if he hopes to give a clear and unmistakable meaning to what he is saying over the radio. That way, his listeners will know exactly how to interpret what he is saying. If he reports, "the vehicle traveled through the neighborhood," he's not really being clear. He's leaving his listeners to interpret "vehicle," "traveled," and "neighborhood," to their own liking. If he reports, "the car sped down the street," he's being a little clearer. The vehicle is now not a bus or a truck but a car, and it's probably speeding. But if he reports, "the red Mustang raced through the school zone on High Street," then there is no ambiguity about what he wants his listeners to understand. The communication is clear and unmistakable. The vehicle is now a red Mustang, and it's definitely breaking the law by speeding through a school zone.

His announcement passed through stages from something ambiguous. which could be interpreted to fit perhaps thousands of situations that day, to something concrete and specific, which could only be interpreted one way. In one part of town, someone watching a bus go by, after hearing the first report, could think that that was the fulfillment. Another person across town, hearing the same report and seeing a Cadillac drive by, could feel that that was the fulfillment. The broadcaster, therefore, would use abstract, ambiguous language if he was choosing to remain unclear and thereby allow the public to interpret his words in various ways.

Astrological speculations and generalizations thrive on such abstract language. Your horoscope might say, "Expect triumph!" But it would never say, "You are going to win the bowling championship!" That would be too specific. On any given day, thousands of people could experience and "fulfill" the former, but only one the latter. Horoscopic speculations, by nature, are full of ambiguous language, which different people can apply to their own situations in different ways. This lack of precision makes astrology laughable to some who don't understand the power behind it. It allows people to make it a joke, or a game—how closely can you match the horoscope's broad statements to the specifics of your life? But others are intrigued by it all and are drawn further inside astrology.

It is unwise to place excessive significance on this abstract astrological counsel because of its ambiguous language. It is unreasonable to think that such broad advice constitutes clear, accurate predictions. I could construct a thousand catchy but ambiguous phrases, such as, "You're going to have a fight today," or, "You're going to receive news from a distant source." I could then meander down the street and say these to the next thousand people I'd meet. Because of my ambiguous phrasing, chances are that my advice could come true for many. Yet that should carry no special significance about me. I'm no prophet. I'm just clever enough to take advantage of you by the gimmick of ambiguous, abstract language.

So it is with astrology. In Los Angeles tomorrow morning, 100,000 people might read in their horoscopes, "You will receive news from a distant source." For thousands of them, that might come "true." But that does not mean the horoscope is making accurate predictions. The language is too broad for that to be considered truly accurate communication. The horoscope is *not* saying, "You will get a letter from IBM in Minnesota about your job transfer." It will not dare to be that specific.

Some people who recognize astrology's use of abstract language just laugh it off. For them, astrology is just a harmless, silly game. But don't forget, there *is* power behind astrology. Despite its limitations, it is nothing to fool with.

Take the case of Elaine and Ed. Generalizations are at work here. Yet that's not all. To fully understand what is going on, we need to consider the use of abstract language *plus* the spirit realm. Ed knew enough about astrology to remember that a strong Venus indicates artistic ability. When he discovered, in their conversation, that Elaine was into some specific artistic disciplines, like dance and painting, he ventured his "guess" to her, probably merely as a conversation piece. And, what do you know . . . ? Elaine knew enough about her horoscope to confirm the suspicion. I'm sure the confirmation impressed both parties and threw a more favorable light upon astrology. Yet from what we now know about this system, it is possible that something other than Ed's memory triggered his recall of this astrological information.

Remember, the horoscopic chart is contact material for mediumship. Get rid of the chart and the spirits have no point of contact with the spokesperson and no way of getting information through to the observer. Yet there are other contact materials as well. You may never have had your horoscope constructed, but you may be like Ed. The abstract astrological knowledge you retain in your memory can be used as contact material. If Ed hadn't read books by, say, Linda Goodman or Alan Leo, he would not have known (point of contact) what a prominent Venus indicates. Because he did, he left himself open to being taken advantage of by the deceptive spirit realm. It is possible that this spiritual realm made use of both Ed's and Elaine's retained astrological knowledge, made the psychic connection, and tied it all together in this specific conversation.

I am not saying that Ed is a spirit medium in the sense that a seasoned astrologer becomes one. I am suggesting that he, and hundreds of thousands of others, have enough "contact material"—retained knowledge of *abstract concepts* of astrology—that they are unwittingly leaving themselves open to receive mental influences from the spirit world. These forces help Ed's mind connect general horoscopic statements with specific incidents and coax him to think that the astrological generalizations themselves are specific and accurate. And when both parties have "retained knowledge" about astrology, the possibility that abstract astrological concepts and advice will be directed into specific conversations relating to specific interests increases dramatically.

The spirit realm operating in connection with the ambiguous language usually accounts for this lesser manner in which astrology "works." It is an attempt to get the casually interested to believe that a speculation or a generalization is that specific something. And if you believe this, you will think that astrology is working. Yet, it is not really "working" at all. Specific incidents are being made to refer back to ambiguous advice. Not what astrology books teach, but the ambiguous language and the deceptive spiritual realm hold the key to this phenomenon. For instance, if your daily horoscope says that you will get into a fight with someone, that could mean things ranging from getting a black eye from a mugger, to a shouting match with your teenager, to hanging up the phone on your husband. Now, many find it impossible to get through a twenty-four-hour period without having some kind of squabble. What if that's you? If you get into a "fight" with someone today, why should you blame astrology for it? *You* are the one with the temper. And astrology's abstract advice can mean almost anything.

Astrology is not prophetic. It is making clever use of ambiguous language and coaxing you into believing that it means something specific. Things like reading horoscope columns and getting astrological character trait readouts from a computer should be shunned. The advice is not specific and can later be used as contact material for influences from the spirit world. Even if it is only your own memory that recalls the advice, you need to realize that it was general and not specific advice or counsel. If horoscope columns and sun-sign paperbacks and those little starscrolls gave specific advice before the fact, and it often came true, then we might want to take notice. But they do not. There is no reason, therefore, to be enamored with this type of counsel.

ELEVEN
HEART EXAM

Wisdom is the principal thing; therefore, get wisdom. And in all your getting, get understanding. Exalt her, and she will promote you, she shall bring you to honor when you embrace her.[21]
Do not forsake wisdom, and she will protect you; love her, and she will watch over you.[22] (Ancient proverbs)

As we begin this chapter, I would like to ask: Can those inviting prescripts about wisdom be placed above the threshold of astrology?

So far, we have explored some new and deeply heartfelt issues. We have unearthed and unpacked many trunks that lay buried in the field of astrology. And what we've unpacked is quite startling. There is not much left of astrology, just a few mathematical calculations.

There is, however, a final aspect of astrology, apart from its mythology and its power, that we should spend some time with. Another form of magnetism draws people to this system. The attraction of its wisdom.

Step outside with me for a moment. Let's take a walk down the street, around the corner, and into a huge laboratory where a student zoologist is conducting some tests. (I agree, a bit off-beat, but it will provide us with a medical metaphor that will be helpful later.)

As we enter this lab, you can see it is huge, comprised of neatly placed tables of various sizes, upon which lie the bodies of animals. There is a rabbit over there, a fox on a table next to it, a small monkey on another, a turtle, a raccoon, a medium-sized dog, and so on. Even a small bear cub lies on a large table off to the side. Yesterday, a team of zoologists carefully removed the hearts from these bodies and placed them in tanks of formaldehyde that sit on countertops in an adjacent room. The catch is that these tanks have not been labeled as to which heart belongs in which body. Today we are witnessing a student being tested to see if he knows which heart is right for each body. Of course, there is only one right and true answer; only one heart fits each body properly. Throughout the day, this student must rely on specific criteria, taking his time, sorting through this and going over that, perhaps examining recent lecture notes, in order to get it right, in order to determine what heart goes with what physique, to pass the test.

Back out on the street, we are often being called upon, in principle, to conduct a similar test. Unfortunately, we are often caught napping when called upon. Perhaps no one has ever told us about the necessity of this test, or if someone did, it was so long ago that we have forgotten. Whatever the reason, we come out the losers. What "test" am I referring to? It is the test of hearts. It is a heart exam that will expose whether a body of knowledge is genuine wisdom or not.

Many are drawn to astrology because it seems to offer a certain wisdom. It claims to know how the world works, and why. People go through life anxious, at odds with the world. Astrology offers a system that seems to make sense, that seems to unlock the secrets of the universe. Many people buy into it for that reason.

But is astrology's "wisdom" true wisdom? That's why we need to do this "heart exam," to test it out. We can discover if astrological wisdom is true wisdom by seeing if its heart is compatible with the heart of genuine wisdom.

The question is, Does the heart of genuine wisdom fit in the body of knowledge we have in front of us? Whether that "body of knowledge" is astrology, fortune-telling, psychology, materialism, or Christianity, we need to see whether its heart is the heart of true wisdom.

To conduct this test we need to have the heart of genuine wisdom in our hands. We need to know what it looks like.

But what do we mean by "wisdom"? And how do we get hold of this heart? In the simplest of terms, I think most persons would agree that genuine wisdom is the understanding of what is right and true, and thus lasting, regarding reality and existence—God, man, the universe. A person with genuine wisdom walks through life understanding what is right and true about life, and how the big questions of reality help answer the little questions of everyday life.

The best example of wisdom I know of is Solomon. If Solomon is famous throughout history for anything, it is for his vast wisdom. As one reads his life story, comes to grips with what he knew, looks at the decisions he made, studies what he wrote, one's breath is almost taken away. Sheer genius. Solomon had such seemingly boundless wisdom that it seems impossible for him to have acquired it on his own. One gets the impression that God himself must have given it to him. And that is precisely what the Bible says: "God gave Solomon wisdom and very great insight, and a breadth of understanding as measureless as the sand on the seashore. Solomon's wisdom was greater than the wisdom of all the men of the East, and greater than all the wisdom of Egypt. He was wiser than any other man. . . . And his fame spread to all the surrounding nations. He spoke three thousand proverbs and his songs numbered a thousand and five. He described plant life, from the cedar of Lebanon to the hyssop that grows out of walls. He also taught about animals and birds, reptiles and fish. Men of all nations came to listen to Solomon's wisdom, sent by all the kings of the world, who had heard of his wisdom" (1 Kings 4:29-34).

Pretty impressive. How would you like to have that boasted about you? Fortunately, Solomon has left a book behind in which we can learn plenty about genuine wisdom: the Book of Proverbs. But that's not all. Solomon was wise enough to realize that future generations would need a method by which to test bodies of knowledge to see whether they were wise. He realized that, as time went on, knowledge would expand. And he knew that a lot of this future knowledge about human nature and spirituality would be misleading, as plenty of it was in his day. Part of his genius shines through in that he realized that if we could recognize the *heart* of genuine wisdom, then anyone, anytime, anywhere, would have the criteria to tell whether a particular body of knowledge extended from it.

From passages in the first nine chapters of the Book of Proverbs, Solomon provides us with a detailed and unmistakable description of the heart of genuine wisdom. As the book opens, one can hear Wisdom's impassioned pleas. She is crying out in the street, shouting, longing to be heard by those who have forgotten her. Yet we may find it surprising what genuine wisdom proclaims.

She pleads with us not to chum around with thieves and murderers (1:10-19). She challenges us to earn an honest living (6:6-15). She cries out against adultery and sexual promiscuity (2:16-19; 5:3-23; 6:24-29; ch. 7). She calls us to have a compassionate understanding of our neighbors (3:27-31). She instructs us to stop lying and cursing (4:24). She commands us to honor our parents (6:20). She urges us to trust, fear, and honor the Lord (3:5, 7, 9).

I expected Solomon's description here to consist of esoteric revelations about the Divine, or secret initiations into the keys of evolved spiritual knowledge. But it is not. What we have here is basically an expanded version of the Ten Commandments.

But there is something even more curious about this passage. If we look closely, we notice that woven within this expansion of the Ten Commandments are many disclosures that moral conformity, not knowledge, is at the heart of genuine wisdom. In fact, looking closely (as our student zoologist must have had to do a few times), we find that it says walking in moral obedience *is* the heart of wisdom. It is a *walk,* not a head trip. This is rather amazing. A person begins to acquire true wisdom only when he or she starts walking through life in harmony with the moral principles described here. The heart of genuine wisdom leads me, the searcher for authentic answers, in truly virtuous living.

Solomon is telling us that, in order even to begin to be led by what is truly wise, a person must start by following the leading of the heart of genuine wisdom. Solomon refers to this as having a healthy fear of what God has said. To have a "healthy fear" of God is to believe enough to obey him across the board, knowing that it is for my well-being. Because he created me, God knows what will benefit me. And this is why Solomon goes on to say, in Proverbs 9:10, that "the fear of the Lord is the *beginning* of wisdom." If I am after genuine wisdom, therefore, I should start by following this moral blueprint. We have discovered the heart of genuine wisdom: moral conformity to what God has said.

This may be upsetting to some. People don't want to hear about moral blueprints. It would be much nicer if genuine wisdom did not demand this of them, they think. But wisdom is not found in a universal grab bag of amoral, anything-goes knowledge about human nature. It starts, we are told, with moral commitment.

We are now ready to start comparing the heart of genuine wisdom with the heart of other "wisdoms" like astrology to see if these hearts are harmonious. Immediately we find something more like a glaring contrast than a similarity. In astrology, we find a curious *lack* of moral injunctions at its heart. And this lack of moral injunctions, the heart of astrology, is harmonious with those of other occult practices but not with the heart of genuine wisdom. Therefore, the body of astrological knowledge cannot be genuine wisdom.

Yet the occult hearts are similar in another way—so alike that they might as well be one heart. This is in their heart presuppositions, their assumptions about life, about reality and existence.

The astrological costume differs from that of, say, the ouija board or numerology, but its underlying presuppositions—that which is assumed to be true about God, man, and the universe *before* a certain structure of explanation can be contrived—are compatible with those in the rest of the occult. All occult crafts live together non-antagonistically at the root or heart level.

So what do these practices agree on? What underlying views do they share? Just this: They explain reality and existence in any way *except* the biblical way. All occult teaching, no matter how diversely coded in Western, naturalistic/scientific nomenclature, can be traced back to this: explain God, man, and the creation in any way *except* the biblical way. This is so important to understand. That is the heart of the world of the occult, which includes the field of astrology.

We will discuss this a bit more in the next chapter. Yet it does not take a college education to realize that this "heart" of the occult is not the heart of genuine wisdom. It is a heart antagonistic toward the heart of genuine wisdom. This may help explain why "wisdom" in the occult is thought of as a grab bag of knowledge that has nothing to do with morality. The occult has to have some "satisfying" explanation as to what wisdom is, so it comes up with a head trip, not a moral walk. Genuine wisdom, however, does not begin with esoteric occult knowledge and misexplanations of God, man, and the universe. No wonder the world of the occult has so many diverse fields. If you have a hidden agenda that says, "Explain how a TV camera works in any way except the right way," why, the possibilities for misexplanations are so assorted that almost anything goes. But there is only one way to explain it properly; so, too, with God, man, and the universe.

As was mentioned earlier, ours is an age disinterested in moral blueprints. And nowhere is there found a greater dislike for true morality than in the occult. And now we see why. Its disciples are not taught about it. True moral principles are therefore excluded from the occult's solutions to our underlying, spiritual needs, and "knowledge" and "experience" are said to be the solution. Yes, the occult does have a view toward spirituality. The problem is that this view provides no solution for that inescapable spiritual part of me that is morally inclined. It ignores my moral side. And the solution it does give comes out of a false view of God, man, and the universe.

Everyone has a spiritual inclination, no matter how varied or simple. This is evident in the moral motions inescapably present within us, those annoying little jerks of conscience that tell us some things are right and other things are wrong. These moral nudges, however varied, exist in all humans. They are inescapable and, therefore, should not be ignored but attended to with proper care. This means that, in order to truly exercise our spiritual nature, we must have a commitment to moral principles. This is precisely why Solomon teaches us that true spirituality *cannot* be exercised apart from true morality. Truly spiritual answers must have the power to help us out morally; they must deal properly with our moral dilemmas. And occult knowledge is impotent in this area. It can only ignore our moral needs, implying that we can exercise our spiritual nature apart from morality. But this is really cheating; it is not being consistent with human nature.

If the "wisdom" I am into does not have the heart to help me out where it counts the most—morally—then I'm really getting nowhere, for such wisdom lacks the crucial element of spiritual *power*. I will have more to say about spiritual power in the following chapters. Yet because we are conditioned to ignore this key area of human nature, there is nothing left for us to cling to. As a result, we tend to fall in love with methodologies that just give out information about the human soul while saying nothing morally to us.

Our culture has taken a liking to the titillating feeling given to us by amoral knowledge and experience as replacement answers to the big questions. Thus, the many-costumed body of the occult has become a fair mistress these days. She feels good. She strokes our spiritual/moral side, seemingly without demanding anything right or wrong from us. What more could we ask? If there is a greater lie I would like to know what it is. She only seems to be undemanding. She only seems to offer a lifestyle of freedom and liberty. She only seems to offer true spiritual answers to the big questions. She only seems to satisfy our spiritual hunger.

We saw earlier that, at its deepest and fullest expression, she makes insidious demands of her lovers, demands that are far more confining than the moral principles that make up the heart of genuine wisdom. She makes such demands because she is not spiritually true. Creeping bondage is her charm upon the occultist as he or she, though probably living a most pleasing life with her for a season, slowly backslides into the grip of a rationale that is spiritually impotent. It is a rationale that cares not for a person's well-being, but steals one's uniqueness as a human being by negating the moral motions that are an integral part of human spirituality.

The occult demands more than you think it does. Yes, it seems spiritual, but it is evil-spiritual. Not even one cell in its many-costumed bodies has the nature of genuine wisdom.

True spirituality seeks to awaken our consciences, to help us out of moral problems rather than to ignore them and thereby get us into worse shape. It knows how to ease our suffering and dry our tears. It looks out for our well-being. It will point its searchers to the heart of genuine wisdom as the beginning of the path. Thus, the inviting prescripts about genuine wisdom that began this chapter cannot be placed above the threshold of astrology, or of any occult practice, and be true. In the following chapters we will take a glimpse at the path where they are true and look at the door over which they are written.

TWELVE
THE ALTERNATIVE

Truth is a deflector from error. It is a sign pointing: "Go another way, for your safety." Remove the deflectors and one can easily wander the wrong trail for years and never know it. It is clear that in its literature the religion-science of astrology leaves many prime details buried. Or, in keeping with the metaphor above, this craft seems to feel no need to post the signs. Yet, as we have looked honestly at the subject, the nature of astrology has changed *completely.*

Many people would never have entered the astrological heavens if the signs pointing to the ancient gods, the deceptive beings, and the false spirituality were posted, as they should be, in its literature. For the almost eight years that I studied astrology, I had no idea whatsoever that it contained so much error and deception. As a youth, I grew up wanting nothing to do with the devil. Yet here I was tricked into spending years of sincere searching for truth within a kingdom of deception because the barriers of protection against the gods, the spirits, and the non-genuine wisdom were down. The signs saying "Go another way" were missing. The traveler was not kept safe. I was seeking truth, genuine wisdom, not tricks. I wanted the true Voice at my ear, not that of deceitful beings full of specious promises. I wanted authentic answers, not mythological explanations. Finally, in July 1976, I was able to accept what the true Voice had to say. It got through to me, despite all the dense confusion produced by the practice of astrology. It was the Voice of authentic answers.

Authentic answers are true-to-who-God-is answers, true-to-what-creation-is answers, true-to-who-we-are answers. Authentic answers quiet that unrelenting nag in our hearts. Authentic answers satisfy that inner hungering. It is marvelous that such answers exist. Without them life is superficial and meaningless.

Earlier I implied that the Voice of authentic answers is heard more clearly than anywhere else in the pages of the Bible. Yet people react in strange ways to the Bible. It is said that the Bible is the best-selling of all books and perhaps the least read. How odd that it sits with dust on our shelves rather than with humility on our laps. Could a person become a chemist or a zoologist, or even an astrologer, without reading the required books? Why have we taken this impossible notion of education and brought it to bear upon the Bible? Somehow, we must feel that we are able to learn what is in this book by some sort of mystical biblical-literary osmosis. This is dumb. We don't look at learning other knowledge this way. Everyone seems to have an opinion about the Bible, yet even among those who claim to follow its teaching, many never read it. It is respected, honored, but ignored.

Yet authentic answers to the big questions are found there. I mentioned earlier how it irked me when people would mock astrology without knowing much about it. Many do the same thing with the Bible, and this saddens me far more since I have studied both. It is the Bible, not astrology, that rings with authenticity.

We are not talking about religion here. Thinking of the Bible only as a religious book is enough to scare anybody. Think of it as a personal letter. A close friend, even if you've forgotten about him, has sent you valuable information about life—only this close friend happens to be the Creator of the universe. Or think of it as a document from a research corporation, containing the exact answers your company needs.

Some people won't read the Bible because they let others tell them what is in it, but others could be wrong. Other people won't read the Bible because they feel it is beyond their comprehension. Yet not even a mortal with a vital message to communicate sends an unintelligible letter. Would our Creator, then, give us unfathomable letters regarding the big questions, and convolute them so that only a select, initiated few could decipher them? Would he not want them to be read and easily understood by everyone, so that anyone, anytime, anywhere could understand what's going on? It is reasonable to expect a creator to know what is going on with the thing he has created and be able to explain that. So, shouldn't we expect the Creator of our life to know what is going on and to be able to tell us, simply? This is precisely where the Bible fits in.

Without the Bible we are in a real mess. Without that communication from God to us, we have only the universe from which to infer things about God and life. The problem with this is that the universe, because of its subpersonal nature, cannot talk. It cannot articulate what is going on. No sunset or shooting star or puppy dog, no earthquake or flood, is going to cough up authentic answers. But our Creator, the personal-infinite God, can.

In biblical statements we are told exactly what we need to know—not too much, not too little. God knows our need—that we have these big questions that need answering. And he knows that the universe, in itself, cannot answer our spiritual questions. Yet our Creator wants the nag in our hearts quieted, the inner hunger satisfied. And so he has provided us with the revelation of these answers, which are bound together in the one volume that has come to be called the Bible. It is the book of authentic answers for genuine seekers.

Now I know that at this point many people are going to have a hundred complaints against believing what the Bible says. Many well-meaning people have heard the damaging reports that have been uttered against this book. I am not going to discuss these arguments. But let me offer you this to meditate upon as we proceed. Perhaps the insinuations against the Bible have been disseminated, for the most part, by those same methodologies that have this as their heart: explain reality and existence in any way except the biblical way. In other words, if you're going to explain things in any way except that way, you might as well slander *that way* along the way. In any manner possible, get folks to distrust it. If this makes sense to you, I am simply going to ask you to give the Bible a chance. You may be pleasantly surprised at what it has to say to you, as we look at some of its key truths in the following pages.

THE BEGINNING

To explain "what is," God must do some preliminaries. He must reveal some hidden yet foundational truths about reality and existence. He must first provide us with correct understanding of the presuppositions upon which the true explanation is to be built. He must, therefore, share with us how "what is" actually began and became "what is." He would have been most unfair with us if he had not done this; we would be forever grasping at straws to find this needle in the universal haystack. Thus, the book begins as any good text does—at the beginning, by slowly describing God and defining the universe and its creatures. "In the beginning God created the heavens and the earth" (Genesis 1:1). This first sentence of the Bible is the first line of authentic answers. It reveals what we are to initially accept as true concerning God, that he is Creator; and concerning the universe, that he made it. After this opening, we quickly arrive at some details of God's creation of light, the sun, the moon, stars, the earth, trees, vegetation, birds, fish, cattle, and Adam and Eve.

Here we see that a time existed when life was not cruel, as it is today. What we might today call the evils and the injustices of the world did not exist then. It was very quiet and peaceful. Knowing this foundational beginning is a necessary key to understanding properly what is going on today. For, what God created was "good."[23] Indeed, "it was very good."[24] There was no evil in the world. No pain existed then, no sorrow, no war, no manipulation, no alienation between God and man or between Adam and Eve, no deceit, no death. In what God makes there is nothing but good. For he is a good God. He made a good creation.

Most special of all during this time was that Adam and Eve lived in a *personal relationship* with their Creator. This personal relationship was made possible because he is a person and created them as persons. When he created them, he gave them *life* as persons, not *existence* as a blade of grass or a donkey, but *personal life*. And thus there could be this person-to-person relationship not only between Eve and Adam, but between them and God. "Personal relationship" with God means that they had contact and communication with him similar to the manner of children living with their parents. I know this is hard to believe today, in our modern world of narcissism and alienation. But it was that real. There they knew of his presence.[25] They knew him in such a way that no one could make them believe that he did not exist! The three of them talked freely with one another. They all had personal fellowship together. Nothing separated them. This is how all things began. It was good. And it is a foundational authentic answer for properly understanding life today.

Suddenly, with great discord, on the heels of what is good, terror strikes! *Something occurs that God did not create:* the "fall" of Adam and his wife. It is easy to become muddled about life by not knowing this. We start to blame God for all of the evil and cruelty around. But God *did not* create this, though in his compassion for us he has done something about it, as we shall shortly see.

The "fall" occurred when what is known as *sin* entered into the lives of our first parents, Adam and Eve. *Sin* uncoupled the primary human family from God, and consequently did the same for the entire human family, including us, their children. When sin became a part of their lives, not only were they uncoupled from God, but their lives began producing the disgusting things that we have in our world today. Unpleasant things like hatred, discord, jealousy, rage, selfish ambition, dissension, and envy began then, slowly, at first. God did not intend that societies and cultures, tribes and nations, individuals and families grow up without personally knowing him and the peace and harmony that this experience produces. But that is what has happened.

Sin entered the human family and brought with it these and other nasty side-effects. Sin has set up an impenetrable wall, tall above our eyes, keeping us from seeing God on the other side. And so we go about our business, doing the things we do, without realizing that the God of true peace is there.

Human discord began in that historical moment, in the Garden of Eden when our first parents sinned and lost touch with God. It was brought on by humans, and it continues today because of us. If we hope to build an intellectual structure that rightly interprets "what is," we must accept these foundational truths, not just because the Bible says them, but because they are truths that fit what is going on today in a way that no other answers do.

THE PROBLEM OF SIN

Sin now quarantines us from God, our Creator. Thus, we, unlike Adam and Eve, are talked out of believing that he exists. As we saw earlier, God had warned them, quite clearly, of the consequences of listening to other voices.[26] He did not play games with them. He posted the warning signs. For he knew that in being misled by deceptive voices they would sin, and that the consequence of this would be to be cut off from him who had given them life in the first place. If they went wrong they would be cut off from him whose life was sustaining them. And *that* would mean inevitable death. So he warned them. He longed for the human family to remain alive, free from sin and death. He wanted them to remain in a personal fellowship with him. So he gave them a simple direction to follow. (Some wrongly believe that God's directions are the mean-spirited demands of a cruel oppressor when actually the opposite is true. He posts the warning signs *because* of his compassion and care for us, that we may live peacefully, sheltered from death, in *life* with him.) Unfortunately, Adam and Eve disobeyed, and so do we. Thus the slow-working, fatal venom (sin) that brought about the death of our first parents works in us also.

Of course, this carries the distasteful implication that *everyone* sins and is separated from God by disobedience. For many, this is difficult to accept, probably because this authentic answer is so inclusive; it includes them. They, too, are sinners. Yet, how do we define "sinner"? What are "sins"? Simply put, they are those things that you *know* you should not have done, from things like lies to things like adultery. Who can honestly admit to never doing anything wrong?

When Adam and Eve sinned, they *knew* they had done wrong. They were so afraid that they even tried to hide from God (see Genesis 3:8). The point is that sin cost them God's gentle, parental guidance. Immediately this left a huge void in their lives, and sin's dominion quickly moved in to set up its harsh rule over them. Sin led them away from their gentle Father into bondage to a cruel oppressor, a harsh taskmaster who, in the end, pays wages not of life but of death. The real problem with sin, therefore, is that it isolates us from our Creator, who is now our life, and we die as the result.

Sin first kills us spiritually (we become unaware of God), then physically. The day they sinned, Adam and Eve died spiritually. Years later, their bodies inevitably died, for no spiritual life remained to sustain them; it had dwindled to the point where all their bodies could accomplish was to breathe a final breath and expire. This is why you will find authentic answers teaching that we who live and breathe and walk and work and eat our meals and communicate in society are "dead." Not buried-in-the-grave dead, yet, of course, "dead" in that we lack "what actually constitutes life, i.e., a (personal) relationship with God."[27] Biblical passages teach that humans are "dead in transgressions and sins";[28] "dead" in that we are "alienated from the *life* of God."[29] This deadness is not just a theory.

I literally saw this deadness once, in living human beings, right before my very eyes. It terrified me. I'll never forget it. It was about 1971, and I was stretched out on the sofa in my living room, listening to some Neil Young on the stereo. Dave (my roommate), Frank, Danny, and some other friends were in the adjacent dining room playing cards—a normal event at our flat. It was late, and I had been fading in and out between a half sleep and the music on the stereo, not at all bothered by the good-natured banter and the cigarette smoke of close friends in the next room. I suppose I'd been lying there an hour or more. For some reason I suddenly sat up *and things just looked strange;* the music even had the most peculiar sound to it, like I'd never heard before or since. I thought I'd better get up, so I took a few steps to the end of the sofa and turned right to enter the room where my friends were seated around a large oval table playing cards. I was stunned! There they were, laughing, chatting, and carrying on—and they were all dead! I'm not joking. I'm serious. Everyone at that table was dead! You could not have paid me 10 million dollars to believe otherwise. I remember one or two of them looked especially corpse-like, chatting with cigarettes lilting between dead lips, with the smoke drifting in front of their lifeless faces. I stood there in that doorway shocked. (As I write this line to you tonight, fifteen years later, I recall that the Neil Young song "Southern Man" was playing on the stereo. And in that song is the line, "Don't forget what the 'Good Book' says.")

I really couldn't believe what I was seeing. It was as if a veil was pulled off my eyes for a few seconds. To this day I don't know why I was meant to see this. I remember how my stomach turned and my mind warped and I fell on the sofa, trying to shake what I'd just seen—a little community of dead people, my friends, playing cards.

Even the most hardened individuals can sense this deadness in themselves at times. And many who are really sensitive to it try to ignore it, hoping it will go away. Others structure their lives full of activities and excitement, hoping to flee the experience of the deadness that inhabits the moments of stillness. Others who sense it often try to get in touch with it, hoping to define it, to come up with the authentic answer for it. Theories like angst, or nihilism, therefore, appear. Yet it is not only in philosophy that this issue is tackled. It is also prevalent in the arts, especially in music.

So when you hear, for example (to use one of my old favorites), the Four Tops' old song, "Baby, I Need Your Loving," you come across the line, "This loneliness inside me makes me feel half-alive." This thing of being "half-alive" has a peculiar familiarity, and as I hear it I muse, "So the Four Tops have been there too." The lyric becomes a confirmation, not just of something that I am experiencing individually, but of something that everyone experiences in one way or another. This sense of being "half-alive" is an indication of our personal and spiritual alienation, separation, from God. (Actually, a sense of this deadness should be regarded as a safeguard in our being. It is not wrong to sense the deadness; that may be the first step away from the dead end.)

Let's stop and review here for a moment. For you can see how completely different authentic answers are from the information that comes out of astrology. This chapter presents us with some basic, beginning authentic answers: the creation of all things by the infinite-personal God, the falling away (sinning) of male and female from God, and its inevitable consequences—the deadness and discord, the lifelessness.

In the last chapter we saw that astrology cannot provide these authentic answers because, as a field in the world of the occult, it does not have the heart of genuine wisdom. It misexplains reality and existence. Now the world of the occult is comprised of many fields of this false spirituality. Some of these are anthroposophy, black and white magic, charming, death magic, fetishes, fortune-telling, letters of protection, magical healing methods, mental suggestion, mind development, necromancy, numerology, ouija boards, palmistry, past life recall, rod and pendulum, Rosicrucianism, sorcery, spiritism, superstition, tarot, the Urantia book, witchcraft or Wicca, yoga, and astrology. We have seen that at the heart or presuppositional level these practices come out of an erroneous way of seeing God, man, and the creation. Remember, this erroneous way of seeing is: explain God, man, and the creation in any way except the biblical way.

If we wanted to put a definition upon these ways of misexplaining things, presuppositionally, we would have two choices. They are called pantheism and polytheism. Indirectly, these account for the "theology" of astrology. Yet over the millenia and up into recent history it would be more correct to say that the occult begins with an odd union of these two ways of seeing. This mating has produced various degrees of what has been called animism and monism. And most recently, the four of these misexplanations are getting together (a sort of antispiritual genetic tinkering, I suppose) to produce a child for the twenty-first century. This grotesque creature, or beast, it should probably be called, this gross distortion of wisdom, has lately been given a new name: New Age thinking. This child-beast has risen out of the Enlightenment union of these four ways of misinterpreting reality and existence. They all deny the validity of genuine wisdom. This is why New Age teaching gives us the erroneous modern ideas that the universe is being guided by "helpful" elemental spirits and evolved masters who dish out seemingly endless platters of experiences and knowledge that, when we digest it all, is supposed to lead us in a spiritual evolution to discover the "oneness" of all, which we had supposedly forgotten. And this is why modern astrology will indirectly, though harmoniously, refer you to this way of seeing reality rather than the authentic way, which is that God created us and that our sins have separated us from him. This is also why, sadly, the modern astrologer will nod his head in agreement with this "New Age" view that spiritual evolution is our salvation. For modern astrology is sympathetic with the teaching of this child-beast.

It is not necessary, for our studies here, that we discuss these four ways of misinterpreting things. What is necessary is that we realize that they account for the "theology" of astrology as well as that of the rest of the occult. And because every body of occult knowledge denies true morality and comes out of a mis-explanation of life, none of them can be considered true wisdom.

Can we not see that what we have with us today in astrology and in the rest of the occult New Age teaching is merely a consistent extension of the deception from the serpent in the Garden? "Has God really said you will die?" he says. "You will not surely die. You will be like God" (Genesis 3:4-5). But the facts are that we all die and that none of us is God.

A friend of mine once heard a professor tell him a very wise thing, "If your theology doesn't fit the facts, change your theology." Yet too many people do just the opposite. They ignore the facts and cling to an erroneous theology. I suggest that, since our poly/pantheism, even when extrapolated into the twenty-first century, doesn't fit the facts, we should scrap it. That we will not die, that we will be like God, that all is "one" sounds great. But it doesn't fit the facts. We all die, none of us is God, and there are distinctions between things. Modern occult thinking is merely the deception that began in the Garden outworked in our day in a way in which we today can assimilate and understand it.

What disgusts me the most is that this deception is so wicked as to play upon an innocent person's desires to do good. The following is quoted from "War on the Saints" by Jessie Penn-Lewis:

In Genesis we have the simple story of the garden, with the guileless pair unaware of danger from evil beings in the unseen world. We find recorded there Satan's first work as deceiver, and the subtle form of his deception. We see him working upon an innocent creature's highest and purest desires, and cloaking his own purpose of ruin under the guise of seek-

ing to lead a human being nearer to God. We see him using "good" to bring about evil; suggesting evil to bring about supposed good. Caught with the bait of being "wise" and "like God," Eve is blinded to the principle involved in obedience to God, and is deceived.

Goodness, therefore, is no guarantee of protection from deception. The keenest way in which the devil deceives the world . . . is when he comes in the guise of somebody, or something, which apparently causes them to go God-ward and good-ward. He said to Eve, "Ye shall be as gods," but he did not say, "And ye shall be like demons."[30]

And even today we see the devil's distorted wisdom in New Age teaching that preys upon the unsuspecting, insidiously working upon the sincere desires of people to find authentic answers to the big questions.

If you have been involved in astrology or another occult practice, you know how the truth of it seems to slip away just when you think you've got it. Its answers just aren't quite satisfying enough; they simply aren't "working" as powerfully as you thought they would. You want another experience and more knowledge. Then when you get these, they too wear off. They're not lastingly satisfying. And so you search for more. And on and on and on it goes. I suggest that we turn and test the Bible's answers further.

THIRTEEN
THE PURCHASE

The fall had occurred. Sin was now pervading human nature, with disfellowship from God and death as the result, not to mention that cultures were now being grown in the soil of unrest. What then was God, being good, to do? The race he had made now roamed lost. Was he simply to watch now, helpless, as they wasted away? Surely this would not speak of goodness in God, but limitation.[31] What would have been the sense of creating us in the first place if, when we got into trouble, he could not help us?

Being good, and unlimited in power and means, God immediately undertakes the work of rescuing Adam and Eve, and us in the process. Thus begins the center-most biblical theme: God has a plan, he has provided the way for sinful, separated, suffering, deadened humanity to come back to "life" by reentering into a personal relationship with him. Progressively, line by line, throughout the pages of biblical statements, God discloses this plan. From Genesis onward the reader sees the plan unfold more and more clearly, until there can be no mistaking it. Whether one accepts it or not is a different story, but there is no mistaking his plan: I will send someone to rescue you from sin and death and bring you back to life; this someone is Jesus Christ.

LIFE IN THE SON

It is clear that, if we sinned away "life," in order to live again we would have to get "life" back. This is where Jesus Christ, God's Son, comes into the picture. It is in him that we can get life back. For he is Life. Let's unpack a bit of what is hidden in this truth. Remember, the center-most authentic answer is that God, not anyone else, has the plan and the power and the means to retrieve us. Humans cannot do it. Being finite and limited, we cannot produce anything eternal for ourselves. It is silly to think we could give ourselves divinity or eternal life. Whatever we build decays. All our relationships inevitably end. The cold fact is that we sojourn seventy or so years upon this earth and then we perish. If we are ever to receive anything eternal, it needs to be given to us by some order of Being who has it to give. This Being, of course, is God. Yet God must have the way to accomplish this. And the way turns out to be, not a batch of knowledge, but a person—Jesus Christ (see John 14:6). More technically, it is "through the *redemption* that is in Jesus Christ"[32] that we are reunited with our Creator.

Redemption is a big word, yet it has a simple truth behind it. To redeem is to rescue, to free, to buy back, to ransom. From what are we rescued?

Biblical statements give no pretty picture of sin, or of one's rescue from it. Sin chains us in bondage on death row. It owns us. It is a cruel, oppressive master, depriving us of life. It is right that these biblical pictures of sin are so horrifying. For sin is a terrible evil in the world, so deceitful that it is nearly impossible for us to recognize that we are enslaved and unlifed by it. Now if someone could be found who could ransom us from the slave market of sin, absolutely and with no cheating—if someone could buy us, paying whatever the necessary price—only then would we be freed. The one who freed us would be known as our redeemer, and his work would be called redemption.

It can also be said that at the time of our redemption we would immediately realize that we had entered into a personal relationship with our redeemer, even if we had previously not known of his existence. This biblical image of redemption and its implications is similar to the history of slaves in many nations. If you were a slave in the 1600s and someone paid the high dollar necessary to buy your freedom, then that person would be known as your redeemer. And you would immediately realize some sort of personal relationship with the one who had redeemed you, even if, previously, you had never known of your redeemer's existence. This is precisely how it is between God and the sinner. The sinner can be redeemed from sin. And upon this redemption from sin, he or she immediately becomes aware of entering into a personal relationship with God the Redeemer,[33] Jesus Christ. Thus, "through the redemption that is in Jesus Christ" we get life back.

THE MORAL PROBLEM
In the Eastern religious thinking that underlies much of astrology and other areas of the occult and New Age thinking, we find two major ways of explaining the separation between God and humanity: metaphysical and epistemological.

The metaphysical explanation says that my alienation from God stems from my smallness. I am so little, so insignificant, so finite, when contrasted with the reaches of the universe and the divine. The Supreme Being is so big, so infinite, so past finding out. I, therefore, need to grow big enough spiritually to gain divinity. And so I shall master whatever esoteric disciplines and meditations are necessary to increase me in spiritual bigness sufficiently to put divinity in me; or, as some schools teach, to allow me to discover the divinity within myself.

The epistemological line of thought holds that my separation from God stems from my lack of knowledge of him. I know so little, perhaps nothing, about the Supreme Being. And so I need to tediously investigate all knowledge, study the masters of the world's religions, meditate upon Eastern thought, and peruse the occult. Eventually, this wealth of "knowledge" accumulating in me will one day unite me with the Big Whoever, or I may discover that I was "one" with it already.

Much can be honestly discussed: about our littleness before God and our pint-size knowledge of him. But our real problem is not a matter of metaphysics or epistemology, but of morality. Being separated from God is a moral problem. And Jesus Christ came to fix it. He alone has power enough to do so. Occult knowledge is impotent against this problem.

Morals pertain to one's personal behavior as compared with God's character. Right off we see a problem. God's character is perfect and sinless; my behavior is flawed and loaded with sins. The moral problem began in the beginning. Our first parents simply misbehaved. They disobeyed a clearly understood directive, and that was morally wrong. It was sin, it stung them mortally, and they died. And thus we die. Thank God that he can fix this moral problem of our deadness. He has provided the solution, not in a metaphysical shot in the spirit or in epistemological enlightenment, but in the death and resurrection of the Redeemer, Jesus Christ.

Through Jesus Christ we can escape our moral problem. Because of Jesus, life no longer has to be a dead-end street. Through him we can be made alive to God and aware of his presence. It is not knowledge that we have lost, we have lost our *personal relationship* with God our maker, and thus we need to regain that. And so it is not words or teachings or mantras or TM or yoga that we need; neither is it clever instructions coupled with mystical experiences from spirit guides. We need *power*. Power to give us life again. Power that can conquer death.

At one time or another, at least in Western culture, I suppose everyone has heard that Jesus Christ made "the way" for us to receive this power to come back to life when he died on the cross for our sins. But what does that mean? It seems so odd a thing. Why doesn't God just zap us back into a personal relationship with himself? Why the necessity of Jesus' violent death on the cross? It is all rather repulsive, especially in our glossy Western culture.

THE VITAL NECESSITY OF JESUS CHRIST

As a direct result of Adam's disobedience, his personal relationship with God, and thus his life, was lost. It might be argued, therefore, that the opposite of this would effect the cure; that, as a direct result of Adam's subsequent obedience, his personal relationship with God, and thus his life, could be regained. In other words, by a sort of "*self*-redemption" Adam could nullify the bad results himself, by turning around and becoming obedient forever. Instead of walking away from God, let him walk toward God. *He* tore himself away, let *him* restore himself. This sounds feasible, and in most cases it would work. But in this case it would mean that there would have to be more power in Adam's subsequent obedience than in his previous disobedience. Thus, the principle of "doing it himself," applied to this specific case, cannot work. For Adam is now "dead." He has no power left.

Adam has given himself a mortal wound, against which he and his knowledge and his actions are powerless, impotent. He is like the suicidal girl who in one last powerful burst of aggression leaps to her death; on the way down she is powerless to restore what she has just sacrificed—life. Thus, Adam's subsequent obedience, which now takes place while he is dead, cannot be more powerful in effect than was his disobedience. In other words, Adam can never act more powerfully than when he conquered himself in the Garden of Eden. The overwhelming power in Adam and Eve's seemingly remote driplet of disobedience long ago is the most powerful thing man will ever do to, or for, himself. We are now dead. We are powerless against our moral problem. We cannot *redeem* ourselves; we cannot give ourselves life. We have jumped to our deaths. We have not merely lost a "sensitivity" through which we could rediscover God; we have surrendered the spiritual life by which we experience him.

In the case of Adam (or us) coming back to life again, it can never be solved by the self-help, human potential methods. Yes, Adam could turn himself around physically, geographically, but not morally. Adam might be able to stop doing some bad things, and this is good. Yet merely being obedient and doing good is not powerful enough to overthrow death. Morally, Adam was paralyzed, in a never-ending coma. The explosion that tore at his being during the Fall was so severe, affecting him (and all of mankind) in so many dimensions other than physical, that even if he could become perfectly obedient forever, Adam still could not undo the effects of what he had already done. In turning away, he had not just gone to another address; he had killed himself. The dead cannot give themselves life again. Dead is dead. It is final.

Life is the power over death. Adam and Eve had given that up. While yet alive they had life—power over death—and could choose to remain alive. But they chose to allow the sting of sin[34] (death) to enter their veins. While alive, they lost life, with nowhere to fall but into the icy hands of death. No action, therefore, in any of Adam and Eve's subsequent obediences that would now take place while they were "dead in sins" could possibly have power enough, life enough, to rid themselves of death. They gave themselves a mortal wound. Death had them. And it has us.

Imagine with me that I live alone on an enormously plush estate whose green hills, meadows, and woodlands cover miles of countryside. I never tire of exploring. While walking deep in the wooded acreage one afternoon, I discover an old, ugly, iron-barred prison, built near the edge of a deep canyon. Curiosity of the unknown gets me to twist the large, rough key in the iron door lock. The door grates open. And with key in hand I step inside the cell's darkness to investigate. Don't ask me why, but I have snapped the door shut behind me, it locks, and I move across a large space to look out the solitary window. The view from there lets me see down into the canyon, into which I toss the key. You may well think me crazy for tossing it out the window and watching it fall into the darkness of the canyon, gone. Suddenly, embarrassment and dread come over me. I am caught. I need that key to get out. But I have thrown it away. Nothing I now do, either through my intellect or my actions, will nullify my foolishness. I can only wait, separated from the life I had once known, until I expire. My problem is not that I have lost "oneness" with the universe; I have forfeited the life I once had.

But what if someone, quite unknown to me, came along with the master key? The one who holds the key of life is God. Jesus Christ is the key to our moral prison.

Jesus Christ was here on earth to remove our sins by dying upon the cross, which in turn would free us from death and give us eternal life by bringing us back into a personal relationship with God. This is what is meant by his *redeeming* us. And it was *his* obedience that made this happen. Quite unlike Adam (and us), Jesus was never disobedient to his Father's will. Therefore, by his obedience he keeps his life and somehow is able to give it to us, to overthrow the death-power of our disobedience. It is Jesus Christ's obedience, not Adam's or mine, that has power enough, life enough, to conquer death.

To say this in the words of the Bible: "Therefore, just as sin entered the world through one man, and death through sin, and in this way death came to all men, because all sinned. . . . Just as the result of one trespass [disobedience] was condemnation for all men, so also the result of one act of righteousness [obedience] was justification that brings life for all men. For just as through the disobedience of the one man the many were made sinners, so also through the obedience of the one man the many will be made righteous. For if, by the trespass of the one man, death reigned through that one man, how much more will those who receive God's abundant provision of grace and of the gift of righteousness reign in life through the one man, Jesus Christ. So that, just as sin reigned in death, so also grace might reign through righteousness to bring eternal life through Jesus Christ our Lord" (Romans 5:12, 18-19, 17, 21). Simply put, Adam's disobedience brought death to all; Jesus Christ's obedience brings those who believe in him to eternal life.

Thus, God could not just zap eternal life back into us. Reality does not work that way. *The way* of redemption has to be consistent with *the way* reality is, in order for it to work. You have to put the key into the ignition in order to drive the car. That's just the way it is. Thus, we had to be purchased by the death of God's Son because that was the only way we could have spiritual life again. Jesus was able to keep his life because he never did anything worthy of dying. And so it was arranged that on the cross he was able to take our place in death and give us his life! In taking the penalty we deserve (death), he makes the way for us to be brought into a new life.

FOURTEEN
OUT OF YOUR WORLD

It may seem odd that we have labored so long to talk about death and life. Yet that is the real issue. Many quarters of the occult constantly discuss how we will live forever. But we can be sure of one thing: nothing less than, or other than, the true and living and eternal God can give us eternal life. Nothing as unreal as myth, or as limited as knowledge, or as finite as a created being can impart everlasting life. In his book *The City of God*, St. Augustine writes quite plainly about this fallacy of thinking that myth or created being can give us eternal life.

No philosopher, I am sure, would dream of discussing whether such gods (myths) can give us immortal life. But, what of those men, some of them extremely learned and acute, who boast of having written useful books of instructions to help people to know why each of the different gods is to be prayed to, and what is to be asked of each, and how to avoid the unbecoming absurdity of asking, like a clown on the stage, for water from Bacchus or for wine from the Lymphae? Would they take the responsibility for a person who, when praying to the . . . gods and asking the Lymphae for wine and getting the answer: "We have only water, ask Bacchus for wine," should rightly say: If you have no wine, give me, at any rate, your immortal life?

Just think of the monstrous absurdity of the Lymphae an-swering with a laugh—for, according to Virgil, they are given to laughter—"O man, do not think that we have the power to give you life (vitam), *when you have just been told that we can't even give you wine* (vitem)!" *(I am supposing that, un-like the demons, they would not try to deceive him.) It is in-deed monstrous and absurd to ask or hope for eternal life from gods like this. Here they (the myths) are so assigned to such tiny and fragmentary adjuncts of our sad and transient life that, when you ask one of them for something in the de-partment of another, you get a situation as a scurrilous em-barrassment on the stage.*

In regards to the gods and goddesses set up by various cities, learned men have discovered and listed what each must be asked for. . . . Just think. If it is a mistake to ask wine of Ceres, bread of Bacchus, water of Vulcan, fire from Lymphae, you can imagine how crazy we ought to think a man who should ask of any of such gods for eternal life.

No human intelligence is so dull as to believe that a wor-ship of such gods can bear any fruit in eternity. . . . Such gods, then, cannot give us eternal life. Not even those who wanted them to be worshiped by the ignorant populace dared to make such a claim. They were content to divide up the oc-cupations of earthly life, and to keep all of their gods busy, as-signed each to a particular job.[35]

The resemblance is striking between the gods in myths, in vogue in Augustine's day, and the gods in myths as they are today in the religion-science of astrology. Names have changed, but their mythological natures are the same, and so are the ramifications of trusting in them. I think that St. Augustine would agree that there is no hope of life in astrology. Unfortu-nately, too many persons believe that there is.

One other illustration may help to clear up some of the con-fusion about what it means to have a personal relationship with the true God. Personally entering into eternal life means some-thing quite different than "sensing" or thinking about what is infinite and eternal.

Let us enlarge the meaning of the cube world from chapter 5.

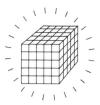

Instead of it representing only the world of astrology, let it represent one's entire life, the total world that wraps up you or me. Let everything outside the walls represent all that is infinite and eternal. The inside of the cube represents you or me with all of our sins, problems, and finiteness.

Imagine with me that one day you were visiting the center-most cube, involved with whatever it is that goes on there. While there, it could be said that you were not able to "sense" the existence of God. If questioned about God, you might even strongly doubt his existence. In fact, while in this center-most cube, whatever you did would be done as though God did not exist or did not matter. You would feel this way because of being surrounded by finite and relative principles.

Some days later, you take a little walk, arriving in one of the outer cubes. Leaning against the outermost wall, because it rubs up against what is infinite and eternal, you are going to have some "sensing" or some thoughts of the God who is there.[36] You may even wonder why you so doubted his existence a few days earlier. It is not long, however, before you move back to one of the center cubes and listen to the thoughts there. Then, still later, you are back in one of the outer cubes thinking that there may indeed be a God. This is the pattern of one's beliefs about God and eternal life—belief, a mind-set, that vacillates between atheism and agnosticism. This is the pattern until one gets outside, until one is rescued by Jesus Christ.

Note carefully: Even if a person presses hard up against the outer edge of an outer cube, momentarily gaining a keen estimation of God's existence, this is not what it means to be in a personal relationship with him. To "enter into" presupposes exiting from someplace. In this case, to enter into a personal relationship with God, we must get outside the cube-world of sin that has us locked in quarantine from God. For this "exiting" to occur there must be the door of escape. This again brings us to Jesus Christ, who is himself the door. The door of escape is another way of talking about the redemption.

The Bible reveals that eternal life begins for a person when his or her sins are taken out of the way. We have already discussed that it was sin which produced death. And that if the "producer" can be eliminated by something greater in power, then death would be done away with and life would return. And we also saw that myths do not have this greater power, nor do I, nor do any created life forms (even angels), nor do we find this power merely in a sensing of God's existence. We are left with God alone. Only his life is this power over death. Thus, he must somehow make his life available to us, using it to produce the necessary power to take away our sins. And he has done this through Jesus Christ dying upon the cross. The cross is then, in a sense, the only door in existence whereby a person can escape sin and live again. This is why it was a necessity.

Not too many days before his death and resurrection, Jesus was speaking to his disciples and to some of the religious leaders of that time about this door he was about to set up. Yet even some of his closest friends misunderstood him.

As was noted, biblical statements from Genesis onward, line upon line, reveal more and more of the details of this plan of God to rescue us. In the Old Testament, God's plan becomes clearer and clearer; then, at last, Jesus comes not only to fulfill the plan but also to reveal the final details of it. But many are still missing the point. The final nail is about to be driven in, to complete the work, and even Jesus' intimate friends, who believed the Old Testament's authentic answers, were having great difficulty comprehending that Jesus was the door of escape. So Jesus, during his last few weeks on earth, labored hard, intellectually, with them, to press the matter home.

Jesus therefore said to them again, "Truly, truly, I say to you, I am the door of the sheep. All who came before Me are thieves and robbers, but the sheep did not hear them. I am the door; if anyone enters through Me, he shall be saved. . . . The thief comes only to steal, and kill, and destroy; I came that they might have life, and might have it abundantly. I am the good shepherd; the good shepherd lays down His life for

the sheep. . . . For this reason the Father loves Me, because I
lay down my life. . . . No one has taken it away from Me, but
I lay it down on My own initiative. I have authority to lay it
down, and I have authority to take it up again." (John 10:7-
11, 17-18, NASB)

This is pretty clear. Yet just hours before his death, Jesus had
to try again to clear up the meaning of his death. It seems that
one apostle was especially confused about the door of redemption. Thomas couldn't figure out what Jesus was doing, where
he was going, or how he (Thomas) could follow him. For Thomas knew that he must follow Jesus, and he wanted to, but he was
confused. Thus Jesus plainly said to him, "I am the way and the
truth and the life. No one comes to the Father except through
me" (John 14:6).

On another occasion, Jesus explained the door of his death in
this way: "Just as Moses lifted up the snake in the desert, so the
Son of Man must be lifted up, that everyone who believes in him
may have eternal life" (John 3:14-15).

Jesus was referring to an Old Testament incident (Numbers
21:4-9) which the apostles knew well. It was a time when Moses
was leading the people of Israel through a desert region. During
this time, the people sinned and, as a result, "venomous snakes"
came into their midst. These snakes, or "fiery serpents," as one
Bible translation calls them, bit the people, and many of them
died. When the people realized that the fiery serpents had come
because of their sin, they went to Moses, admitted their sin, and
asked him to pray that the Lord would take these serpents (the
sting of sin) away. After Moses prayed, the Lord said that he
would do this, but in a peculiar way.

The Lord said to Moses, "Make a snake and put it up on a
pole; anyone who is bitten can look at it and live." So Moses
made a bronze snake and put it up on a pole. Then when any-
one was bitten by a snake and looked at the bronze snake, he
lived. (Numbers 21:8-9)

Jesus compares that pole to his own cross. Sin has stung us,
but there is a cure. Just as the people of Israel had to admit that

they had sinned *before* they could be cured by looking at the bronze serpent upon the pole, so, too, we must first confess that we have sinned and then look to Christ upon the cross. Like them, we too must be willing to stop sinning and leave our sins behind. Biblically, this is called repentance. It simply means that we are genuinely sorry for what we have done wrong and that we have an honest intention to leave those things behind and follow Jesus.

Many balk right here. They simply will not sincerely admit and confess their sins to God. I was like this. I always thought that if I did this—admitted to God that I had done wrong things—that he would then pitch one of those lightning bolts at me, which I mistakenly thought he kept handy behind his ear, and strike me dead. For some reason, I had the mistaken notion that if I *admitted* my sins then God would say, "Aha! Now I can get you!" But I had it all backwards. When in July 1976 I finally got up the nerve to seriously admit to him that I had done wrong, I discovered that just the opposite was true. He was not out to get me, as I had thought. He was waiting to lavish his compassion on me and ease my suffering. I discovered that he was not out to hurt me at all, but that he was hurt *for me* on the cross, and had already taken the first step to help me. The next step was now mine—I had to do something—confess my sins to him, which I did, through many tears, that day in July. A most unusual peace came upon me when I did this, and it has been with me ever since.

God is not our problem. He won't trip us up. He simply knows what our problem is (sin), has pointed it out to us, and says that he has the solution if we want it.

We must look to Jesus. We must humbly lift our searching eyes off of ourselves, but not up into the latitude of the astrological heavens, rather, to that of the hill of Golgotha where Christ died for our sins. Look at it this way:

Suspended between earth and heaven, between finite and infinite, between relatives and absolutes, between creature and Creator, Jesus Christ took the sentence for our sins. His death and resurrection is not a myth, neither is it a "creaturely," or a metaphysical, or an epistemological solution to our moral problem. Jesus' death is the only solution to our moral problem of deadness. And he is waiting compassionately for us to confess our sins to him, so that we can be restored to him and receive life again.

The Roman cross was an excruciating form of capital punishment. It was set upright in the ground, and upon it the accused person died, horribly. When that nailed-up person was Jesus Christ, death on the cross took on a special meaning: our redemption. His death in substitution for my own allows me to enter into a personal relationship with God. When I embrace Christ, the new spiritual life that is ignited within me is an eternal life. If we will believe in him to the point of submitting the rest of our lives to him, we will beat the reaper. May God help us to see.

"This is the testimony: God has given us eternal life, and this life is in his Son. He who has the Son has life; he who does not have the Son of God does not have life" (1 John 5:11-12).

EPILOGUE

What a wave of enthusiasm astrology is. But someone has aptly noted that there is nothing stable in a wave, and as the enthusiasm subsides, disappointment follows. We have seen in this book that this is so with astrology. This is why the truth of astrology darts away at the last moment. Just when you think you've got it, it slips away, because there is no truth to it. Counterfeit truth, yes, but not true truth. Because it is a counterfeit of authentic answers, it satisfies for a season—like counterfeit money does, until the counterfeiter is nabbed—but that's the best it can do. It *must* let you down. That is its nature. To tease. To tantalize. To spoof.

The religion-science of astrology has not raised in us a consciousness of our dignity and significance as human beings, as a special creation made in the image of the true and living and loving God. Rather, it has humiliated us, in our already low estate, in getting us to accept, however unconsciously, that we are myth. Even evolution does better than this. At least in theory it has raised us above the plowing oxen. Not so, astrology. If we extend the actual presuppositions of astrology, without cheating, we find we are created in the image of myth and, therefore, we are nonexistent, raised above nothing. But we are not nothing. We are something. And for this astrology has no answer.

This is where the Bible, with its authentic answers, fits in.

And it is why I have discussed those answers in these closing chapters. Many have never really known what they are. The Bible is not just another book. It is *the* opinion of the universe and beyond, and it is affirmed by God. What more could we ask for? We do not have to guess. The Bible is the yardstick, the rule, the "canon" by which we can understand what is true and what is false, by which we can evaluate what is going on, by which we can measure whatever we believe, and what we are into, and how we look at life, to see if it fits or not. If it fits, we should keep it and develop it. If it does not fit, we should toss it, without feeling cheated. For we are simply chucking what will hurt us.

From the last few chapters, it should be obvious that authentic answers are concerned with something much more profound than simply dropping astrology and the occult. (Dropping the occult is usually impossible anyway, without God's help, for human power is insufficient to overthrow the strong hold of the evil supernatural world that controls those who are deep in the occult.) God wants us to drop *everything* sinful. This is not to say that we drop it anywhere and run; no one is able to do this anyway. We need to drop everything at Jesus' feet and cling to him, asking for forgiveness. We may never have thought like this before. For it means that we are truly able to recognize, perhaps for the first time, what is going on—and in realizing what is going on, to accept it and act upon it.

What is going on is what God has said: (1) he created all things good; (2) we who were once in personal fellowship with him have turned our backs on him; (3) *we* cannot remedy this; (4) he can help us out, only through Jesus Christ; (5) his help is not a patch-up job, a surrendering of only one or two compartments of our life to him; (6), he provides eternal help of a total nature; (7) every part and ounce of our being (spiritual, intellectual, physical) needs to be brought under his lordship; (8) this means forsaking things other than the occult, perhaps lying, stealing, sleeping around, drugs, and so on; (9) it means admitting that these are sins and wrong, and that we are sinners, and confessing *that,* sincerely, to God; (10) once we have seriously realized these things and honestly acted upon them, having arrived at something like, "Lord, help; have mercy on me, a sinner," then God will be faithful and do his part. He will cleanse us from our sins, bring us into a personal relationship with himself, and give us spiritual life. This will bring a conversion from out of the darkness of error and into the light of Truth, and you will know it.

This is the profound perspective of authentic answers. And we learn them in the Bible. It is not that the Bible enables us to think exhaustively about our condition or about God, but truly.

God has not chosen to define things exhaustively. Yet it is often argued that he must have more things to say than what he has put in the Bible. Therefore, as the argument goes, perhaps he says some of these other things in occult systems, like astrology. Well, in order for this to be true, occult knowledge would need to be harmonious with what is in the Bible. And we have discovered that it is not. Therefore, whatever else God may choose to say to us one day, it will be consistent with, not antagonistic toward, the biblical structure. God's voice does not speak in the occult. His enemy's voice does.

We need open minds, but not serenely open to anything. Anything does not go. We must have minds in submission to God's Word, and imaginations under the control of what is real, not mythical. Do you like reading newspaper horoscopes? Does a Libra keychain dangle from your house keys? Do you buy astrology books? Are you thinking about getting your horoscope done? How many times, lately, have you asked someone what his or her sign is? You can never be involved even a little bit with the occult and be in harmony with the will of God; that is like being a little bit pregnant.

There are two deadly side effects to the occult; one is that our minds come under the control of what is not really true, the other is the inevitable marriage to what is evil. This is why astrology should not even be a hobby.

From Genesis to Revelation, the work of the serpent as deceiver of the whole inhabited earth can be seen. His counterfeits are with us, developing throughout every age. The full results of the deception in the Garden of Eden are being worked out in the occult and are gaining ground worldwide as never before in the so-called "New Age Movement."

Over against this we have Jesus Christ, Truth, who stands out as a shining light, powerful and real. How powerful and real? *He made the universe* that we have around us everyday—that's how real and powerful he is. And that's the quality of the help he offers us. And he wants all of me, not just a part. I must confess it all to him, not just the occult parts but also the lying, the cheating, the sleeping around, the drugs, and even those things that I may have never thought of before as sins.

Francis Schaeffer put this well in his second lecture entitled, "Answers to Basic Philosophical Questions." I paraphrase his thoughts here:

Man's dilemma, man's cruelty, is not that which God has made, but is abnormal. And God is a good God. There is a hope of a solution. And the Bible says that God did supply the solution in the person of Jesus Christ and his work for us as he lived for us and died for us on the cross.

The problem is moral, not metaphysical or epistemological. Man is guilty therefore, and not just small. There's nothing wrong with being small, but there is a lot wrong with being guilty, morally guilty, of breaking God's constitution, the law of God. So man is guilty and the solution is in the death of Christ.

We, being made in the image of God, are able to match the defined dilemma to the answers that God gives. The Bible sets forth that these are not theoretical; it sets forth that these are what is. The Bible says these things are really what is, not just abstract answers to our big questions.

But the Bible says something else, that as we accept this Christ, who is the solution to our moral problem, our guilt is gone and actually we can be in fellowship with the personal God who is there. That's the Christian message. Answers like nothing else gives. And not abstract answers, but answers rooted in history. And also that this is what really is. So therefore not only do I suddenly have a set of answers, but as I accept Christ as my Saviour my guilt is removed and I can be in fellowship with the personal God who is there. In short, I am returned to the purpose of my existence, to live in fellowship with the Creator who made me, to love him with all my heart.

As we exchange the silent voices of mythical sweet nothings and the evil voices of spirits' whispering for the voice of the true God, we meet Someone real enough for our realness, One who knows who and what we truly are. In this, the nag in our heart to have the big questions answered is quieted. Our spiritual hunger is satisfied, and we can enter into a personal relationship with our Maker.

May God give us eyes to see and hearts to understand. Mars doesn't rule Aries; Venus doesn't rule Libra; Jupiter doesn't rule Sagittarius; Mercury doesn't rule Gemini. But God the Lord does have rule over all things. Pray to hear the impassioned plea that crackles in his voice. For at the end of all things will be the final judgment, and our eternal destiny will depend not upon the myths we inbreathed at birth, not upon our progress in our spiritual evolution, but upon this: Are we "in Christ," or are we out of Christ?

NOTES

CHAPTER 1

1. Llewellyn George, *A to Z Horoscope Maker and Delineator,* 28th rev. ed. (St. Paul, Minn.: Llewellyn Publications, 1970), 18.

CHAPTER 3

2. Ibid., 9, 11.
3. Margaret E. Hone, *The Modern Textbook of Astrology* (London: L. N. Fowler & Co., Ltd., 1951), 16.
4. George, *A to Z Horoscope,* 15.

CHAPTER 5

5. Edward Tripp, ed., *Crowell's Handbook of Classical Mythology* (New York: New American Library, 1970), Taurus, 546; Pisces, 482; Cancer, 172, 278, 280; Sagittarius, 518.
6. This concept is developed more fully in Francis Schaeffer, *The God Who Is There* (Downers Grove, Ill.: InterVarsity Press, 1967).

CHAPTER 6

7. It is often argued that identical twins have identical horoscopes. This would be the case if both babies were born at *exactly* the same moment. Twins are usually born enough minutes apart to give their horoscopes dissimilarity at key points, which means that each chart would be a bit different in interpretation and each child's life would be lived out somewhat differently.

To build a case for identical horoscopes, it would be better to locate two or more babies born, say, in the same hospital at the same time. Yet this is also rare. In the eight years I practiced this craft, I never came across such charts. And even if you could find children with identical horoscopes and observe them growing up, you would discover a fallacy of astrology. Though their charts would be the same, it is certain that their lives would not be. For example, at age thirty-five, according to astrological logic, they should not have dissimilar major life realities, i.e. in employment, physical characteristics, major life events. Their lives should not be dissimilar if they were children having identical horoscopes. This seems to me to be a strong argument against astrology.

CHAPTER 8

8. Genesis 3:1-6: Now the serpent was more crafty than any of the wild animals the Lord God had made. He said to the woman, "Did God really say, 'You must not eat from any tree in the garden'?"

The woman said to the serpent, "We may eat fruit from the trees in the garden, but God did say, 'You must not eat fruit from the tree that is in the middle of the garden, and you must not touch it, or you will die.'"

"You will not surely die," the serpent said to the woman. "For God knows that when you eat of it your eyes will be opened, and you will be like God, knowing good and evil."

When the woman saw that the fruit of the tree was good for food and pleasing to the eye, and also desirable for gaining wisdom, she took some and ate it. She also gave some to her husband, who was with her, and he ate it.

9. Genesis 2:17: "But you must not eat from the tree of the knowledge of good and evil, for when you eat of it you will surely die."

10. Job 1–2: In the land of Uz there lived a man whose name was Job. This man was blameless and upright; he feared God and shunned evil. He had seven sons and three daughters, and he owned seven thousand sheep, three thousand camels, five hundred yoke of oxen and five hundred donkeys, and had a large number of servants. He was the greatest man among all the people of the East.

His sons used to take turns holding feasts in their homes, and they would invite their three sisters to eat and drink with them. When a period of feasting had run its course, Job would send and have them purified. Early in the morning he would sacrifice a burnt offering for each of them, thinking, "Perhaps my children have sinned and cursed God in their hearts." This was Job's regular custom.

One day the angels came to present themselves before the Lord, and Satan also came with them. The Lord said to Satan, "Where have you come from?"

Satan answered the Lord, "From roaming through the earth and going back and forth in it."

Then the Lord said to Satan, "Have you considered my servant Job? There is no one on earth like him; he is blameless and upright, a man who fears God and shuns evil."

"Does Job fear God for nothing?" Satan replied. "Have you not put a hedge around him and his household and everything he has? You have blessed the work of his hands, so that his flocks and herds are spread throughout the land. But stretch out your hand and strike everything he has, and he will surely curse you to your face."

The Lord said to Satan, "Very well, then, everything he has is in your hands, but on the man himself do not lay a finger."

Then Satan went out from the presence of the Lord.

One day when Job's sons and daughters were feasting and drinking wine at the oldest brother's house, a messenger came to Job and said, "The oxen were plowing and the donkeys were grazing nearby, and the Sabeans attacked and carried them off. They put the servants to the sword, and I am the only one who has escaped to tell you!"

While he was still speaking, another messenger came and said, "The fire of God fell from the sky and burned up the sheep and the servants, and I am the only one who has escaped to tell you!"

While he was still speaking, another messenger came and said, "The Chaldeans formed three raiding parties and swept down on your camels and carried them off. They put the servants to the sword, and I am the only one who has escaped to tell you!"

While he was still speaking, yet another messenger came and said, "Your sons and daughters were feasting and drinking wine at the oldest brother's house, when suddenly a mighty wind swept in from the desert and struck the four corners of the house. It collapsed on them and they are dead, and I am the only one who has escaped to tell you!"

At this, Job got up and tore his robe and shaved his head. Then he fell to the ground in worship and said: "Naked I came from my mother's womb, and naked I will depart. The Lord gave and the Lord has taken away; may the name of the Lord be praised."

In all this, Job did not sin by charging God with wrongdoing.

On another day the angels came to present themselves before the Lord, and Satan also came with them to present himself before him. And the Lord said to Satan, "Where have you come from?"

Satan answered the Lord, "From roaming through the earth and going back and forth in it."

Then the Lord said to Satan, "Have you considered my servant Job? There is no one on earth like him; he is blameless and upright, a man who fears God and shuns evil. And he still maintains his integrity, though you incited me against him to ruin him without any reason."

"Skin for skin!" Satan replied. "A man will give all he has for his own life. But stretch out your hand and strike his flesh and bones, and he will surely curse you to your face."

The Lord said to Satan, "Very well, then, he is in your hands; but you must spare his life."

So Satan went out from the presence of the Lord and afflicted Job with painful sores from the soles of his feet to the top of his head. Then Job took a piece of broken pottery and scraped himself with it as he sat among the ashes.

His wife said to him, "Are you still holding on to your integrity? Curse God and die!"

He replied, "You are talking like a foolish woman. Shall we accept good from God and not trouble?"

In all this, Job did not sin in what he said.

When Job's three friends, Eliphaz the Temanite, Bildad the Shuhite and Zophar the Naamathite, heard about all the troubles that had come upon him, they set out from their homes and met together by agreement to go and sympathize with him and comfort him. When they saw him from a distance, they could hardly recognize him; they began to weep aloud, and they tore their robes and sprinkled dust on their heads. Then they sat on the ground with him for seven days and seven nights. No one said a word to him, because they saw how great his suffering was.

11. Job 1:11: "But stretch out your hand and strike everything he has, and he will surely curse you to your face."

12. Matthew 4:5-6: Then the devil took him to the holy city and had him stand on the highest point of the temple. "If you are the Son of God," he said, "throw yourself down. . . ."

13. For insights as to how biblical statements can be misquoted, see James Sire, *Scripture Twisting* (Downers Grove, Ill. InterVarsity Press, 1980).

14. John 1:1: In the beginning was the Word, and the Word was with God, and the Word was God.

15. John 14:6: Jesus answered [Thomas], "I am the way and the truth and the life. No one comes to the Father except through me."

16. The existence of the devil and *his* angels is affirmed many times in the Bible.

2 Peter 2:4: For if God did not spare angels when they sinned, but sent them to hell, putting them into gloomy dungeons to be held for judgment . . .

Matthew 25:41: "Then he will say to those on his left, 'Depart from me, you who are cursed, into the eternal fire prepared for the devil and his angels.' "

Jude 6: And the angels who did not keep their positions of authority but abandoned their own home—these he has kept in darkness, bound with everlasting chains for judgment on the great Day.

Revelation 12:9: The great dragon was hurled down—that ancient serpent called the devil, or Satan, who leads the whole world astray. He was hurled to the earth, and his angels with him.

17. Mark 5:1-5: They [Jesus and his apostles] went across the lake to the region of the Gerasenes. When Jesus got out of the boat, a man with an evil spirit came from the tombs to meet him. This man lived in the tombs, and no one could bind him any more, not even with a chain. For he had often been chained hand and foot, but he tore the chains apart and broke

the irons on his feet. No one was strong enough to subdue him. Night and day among the tombs and in the hills he would cry out and cut himself with stones. (See also Acts 19:13-17 and Luke 8:26-33.)

18. Perhaps it is because of the severity of harm that we will inevitably incur if we engage in occult crafts that the Bible uses such graphic and offensive images, shockingly, in hope of diverting us from these systems. Or perhaps it is because we are dead to the sting of the pain that we will bring upon ourselves that the Scripture must "stab us awake," hopefully, to the actuality of it.

Deuteronomy 18:10-12: Let no one be found among you who sacrifices his son or daughter in the fire, who practices divination [astrology is a form of this] or sorcery, interprets omens, engages in witchcraft, or casts spells, or who is a medium or spiritist or who consults the dead. *Anyone who does these things is detestable to the Lord . . .* [emphasis mine].

Isaiah 47:10-14: "You have trusted in your wickedness and have said, 'No one sees me.' Your wisdom and knowledge mislead you when you say to yourself, 'I am, and there is none besides me.' Disaster will come upon you, and you will not know how to conjure it away. A calamity will fall upon you that you cannot ward off with a ransom; a catastrophe that you cannot foresee will suddenly come upon you. Keep on, then, with your magic spells and with your many sorceries, which you have labored at since childhood. Perhaps you will succeed, perhaps you will cause terror. All the counsel you have received has only worn you out! Let your astrologers come forward, those stargazers who make predictions month by month, let them save you from what is coming upon you. Surely they are like stubble; the fire will burn them up. They cannot even save themselves from the power of the flame."

19. When we willfully receive the word of the Lord, we happily kick the words of the devil out of our lives. Always this is the case. We are even given a sample of this in the Bible: Acts 19:18-20: Many of those who believed [in Jesus] now came and openly confessed their evil deeds. A number who had practiced sorcery brought their scrolls [the texts of their occult crafts] together and burned them publicly. . . . In this way the word of the Lord spread widely and grew in power.

20. Galatians 5:19-21: The acts of the sinful nature are obvious: sexual immorality, impurity and debauchery; *idolatry and witchcraft;* hatred, discord, jealousy, fits of rage, selfish ambition . . . and the like. I warn you, as I did before, that those who live like this will not inherit the kingdom of God [emphasis mine].

Revelation 21:8: "But the cowardly, the unbelieving, the vile, the murderers, the sexually immoral, those *who practice magic arts,* the idolators and all liars—their place will be in the fiery lake of burning sulphur. This is the second death" (emphasis mine).

Jeremiah 10 gives a startling contrast between fake gods and the true God. Verses 11 and 15 of that chapter well fit the religion-science of astrology: "These gods, who did not make the heavens and the earth, will perish from the earth and from under the heavens. . . . They are worthless, the objects of mockery; when their judgment comes, they will perish."

CHAPTER 11

21. Proverbs 4:7-8, KJV.
22. Proverbs 4:6.

CHAPTER 12

23. Genesis 1:25: God made the wild animals according to their kinds. . . . And God saw that it was good.
24. Genesis 1:31: God saw all that he had made, and it was very good.
25. Genesis 3:8: Then the man and his wife heard the sound of the Lord God as he was walking in the garden in the cool of the day, and they hid from the Lord God among the trees of the garden.
26. Genesis 2:16-17: And the Lord God commanded the man, "You are free to eat from any tree in the garden; but you must not eat from the tree of the knowledge of good and evil, for when you eat of it you will surely die."
27. Ronald Macaulay, "The Christian Mind," in *What in the World Is Real?* (Champaign, Ill.: Communication Institute, 1982), 113.
28. When writing to those who have entered into a personal relationship with God, the Apostle Paul says that they were previously "dead in . . . transgressions and sins" (Ephesians 2:1).
29. In reinforcing the above truth, in his epistle to the Ephesians the apostle writes that those who are outside of a personal relationship with God have their understanding darkened, "Being alienated [separated] from the life of God through the ignorance that is in them, because of the blindness of their heart" (Ephesians 4:18, KJV).
30. Jesse Penn-Lewis, *War on the Saints* (The Christian Literature Crusade, 1977), 1.

CHAPTER 13

31. This truth of our wasting away out of existence after we had sinned, and God not being helpless to do something about it, is beautifully developed in a small book called *St. Athanasius—On the Incarnation* (Crestwood, N.Y.: St. Vladimir's Orthodox Theological Seminary), with an introduction by C. S. Lewis. I don't know if you can find this little work, but I highly recommend it. For the serious student of the Bible, for those serious in their search for truth, this book should be "must" reading. After reading it, you'll feel as if many intellectual cobwebs regarding "the Fall" and the vital necessity of Christ's incarnation have been gently feather-dusted away, allowing much light to shine in the corners. C. S. Lewis says it best, in the introduction to the book: "When I first opened his *De Incarnatione* I soon discovered . . . that I was reading a masterpiece. Only a master mind could, in the fourth century, have written so deeply on such a subject with such classical simplicity."

32. Romans 3:24: . . . justified freely by his grace through the redemption that came by Christ Jesus.

Ephesians 1:7: In him [Jesus Christ] we have redemption through his blood, the forgiveness of sins, in accordance with the riches of God's grace.

Colossians 1:13-14: For he has rescued us from the dominion of darkness and brought us into the kingdom of the Son he loves, in whom we have redemption, the forgiveness of sins.

Hebrews 9:12: He [Christ] did not enter by means of the blood of goats and calves; but he entered the Most Holy Place once for all by his own blood, having obtained *eternal redemption* [emphasis mine].

33. Psalm 34:22: The Lord redeems his servants; no one will be condemned who takes refuge in him.

Psalm 19:14: May the words of my mouth and the meditation of my heart be pleasing in your sight, O Lord, my Rock and my Redeemer.

Psalm 103:2-5: Praise the Lord, O my soul, and forget not all his benefits—who forgives all your sins and heals all your diseases; who redeems your life from the pit and crowns you with love and compassion, who satisfies your desires with good things so that your youth is renewed like the eagle's.

Job 19:25: I know that my Redeemer lives, and that in the end he will stand upon the earth.

2 Timothy 1:12: I know whom I have believed, and am convinced that he is able to guard what I have entrusted to him.

34. 1 Corinthians 15:56: The sting of death is sin. . . .

CHAPTER 14

35. St. Augustine, *The City of God* (Garden City, N.Y.: Image Books, 1958), 119-134.

36. Francis A. Schaeffer, *The God Who Is There* (Downers Grove, Ill.: Inter-Varsity Press, 1968). This excellent book presents the long-forgotten historic Christian case that believing in the true God, the infinite-personal God, is the only sane option to escaping despair, meaninglessness, nihilism; that it is an intelligent and rational and reasonable thing to do; that it is not something like a horrible Puritan superstition, as many today feel. Dr. Schaeffer's development of this truth speaks well to the context of today's world, a world whose view is devoid of true God-consciousness. "In his pride the wicked does not seek him; in all his thoughts there is no room for God" (Psalm 10:4) ". . . and the whole world lieth in wickedness" (1 John 5:19, KJV).

FOR FURTHER READING

Albrecht, Mark. *Reincarnation: A Christian Appraisal.* Downers Grove, Ill.: InterVarsity Press, 1982.

Buell, Jon A., and O. Quentin Hyder. *Jesus: God, Ghost or Guru?* Grand Rapids, Mich.: Zondervan, 1978.

Groothuis, Douglas R. *Unmasking the New Age.* Downers Grove, Ill.: Inter-Varsity Press, 1986.

Koch, Kurt. *Christian Counseling and Occultism.* Grand Rapids, Mich.: Kregel, 1972.

Koch, Kurt. *Demonology, Past and Present.* Grand Rapids, Mich.: Kregel, 1973.

Koch, Kurt. *The Devil's Alphabet.* Grand Rapids, Mich.: Kregel, 1984.

Martin, Walter R. *Kingdom of the Cults.* Minneapolis: Bethany House, 1968.

Martin, Walter R. *Walter Martin's Cults Reference Bible.* Santa Ana, Cal.: Vision House, 1981.

McDowell, Josh, and Don Stewart. *Answers to Tough Questions Skeptics Ask about the Christian Faith.* San Bernardino, Cal.: Here's Life Publishers, 1980.

McDowell, Josh, and Don Stewart. *Understanding the Occult.* San Bernadino, Cal.: Here's Life Publishers, 1982.

Michaelsen, Johanna. *The Beautiful Side of Evil.* Eugene, Oreg.: Harvest House, 1982.

Morey, Robert A. *Horoscopes and the Christian.* Minneapolis: Bethany House, 1981.

Morey, Robert A. *Reincarnation and Christianity.* Minneapolis: Bethany House, 1980.

Van Buskirk, Michael. *Astrology: Revival in the Cosmic Garden.* Booklet. Christian Apologetics: Research and Information Service, P.O. Box 1783, Santa Ana, CA 92702.

GLOSSARY

Worldwide, astrology comprises diverse schools of thought. Definitions of terms vary accordingly. Since this is so, I have provided in this glossary only a basic definition, a general understanding of each term.

ASCENDANT: The sign of the zodiac that is rising in the east at the time of a person's birth; the first house of the horoscope. It is said to signify personality and outer appearance.

ASPECT: Certain angular distances between planets, such as sixty degrees or ninety degrees. Traditionally, these angular distances have been known as "adverse," "favorable," and "neutral." In contemporary astrology they are referred to as "easy" or "difficult."

BENEFIC: An advantageous influence. A favorable planet, i.e., Jupiter, Venus.

BIRTH CHART: A horoscope that is erected, or cast, for the actual time, place, and date of a person's birth.

BIRTH TIME: Exact moment of first breath.

CHART: The actual diagram, or map, used to make astrological delineations. Used as a synonym for *horoscope.*

CONJUNCTION: A planetary aspect of two or more planets when occupying the same degree of longitude. Usually regarded as an adverse or difficult aspect.

CORRELATION: A late-model term for *influence,* because astrology postulates that everything in the universe is correlated.

DEBILITY: The supposed weakened power of a planet whenever it is located in a sign dissimilar to its nature. The opposite of *dignified.*

DELINEATION: The judgment, or reading, or interpretation of the chart or any of its aspects.

DIGNIFIED: The supposed strengthening of a planet's power whenever it is located in a sign similar to its nature. The opposite of *debility*.

EPHEMERIS: The astronomical table or book of tables listing the planet's positions for a given period of time.

ERECT: To cast, or calculate, or compute the chart, using the movements of the planets throughout the signs of the zodiac as the basis for the calculations. The charting, or drawing up, of the planets in the signs and the houses.

EXALTED: See *dignified*.

HOROSCOPE: Strictly speaking, it is the chart plus the delineations, though it is commonly used as a synonym for *chart*.

HOUSES: The twelve spaces of the astrology chart. Each is said to rule over certain things or affairs. It is said, astrologically, that the twelve signs are divisions of time, the twelve house divisions of space. "House" meanings give understanding to different spheres of life to which the "sign" meanings may be expected to relate. See *signs*.

INFLUENCE: The supposed clout that the planets, signs, and houses exert over a person, a group, things, or events (like assassinations or the signing of treaties or the building of the Eiffel Tower). Many terms are used to describe what is behind it, e.g., light, energy, vibration, power, guidance.

MALEFIC: An unfavorable influence. A difficult planet, i.e., Mars, Saturn, Uranus.

MOON-SIGN: The sign of the Zodiac in which the moon is located at the time of a person's birth. In all branches of astrology it is regarded as a powerful significator, believed to largely influence one's personality, as contrasted to the sun-sign, which is said to influence individuality.

NATAL CHART: A synonym for *birth chart*.

OPPOSITION: A planetary aspect of two or more planets 180 degrees apart. Said to be unfavorable or difficult.

PROGRESSED HOROSCOPE: A chart erected for any period or time after a person's birth, say, at age twenty-one. This chart is then compared alongside the birth chart and delineations are made by synthesizing the two.

PROGRESSION: See *progressed horoscope*.

RETROGRADE: A "backward" motion, a backing up, of the planets. The planets *appear* to have this motion in their orbits in consequence of the relative position and motion of the earth.

RISING-SIGN: See *ascendant*.

SEXTILE: Two or more planets sixty degrees apart. A favorable or helpful aspect.

SIGNS: See *zodiac*. "Sign" meanings give an understanding of the different modes of action and behavior. See also *houses*.

SQUARE: Two or more planets ninety degrees apart. An adverse aspect.

SUN-SIGN: The sign of the Zodiac in which the sun is located at the time of a person's birth. Considered the most powerful influence in astrology. Since without the sun nothing would grow or flourish, astrologers have, from this fact of life, pushed the rationale that the sun-sign is the creative principle and personal self-expression. See *moon-sign*.

TRANSIT: The passage of a planet in a progressed chart over the position(s) of a planet(s) in the birth chart, and readings are given accordingly.

TRINE: Two or more planets 120 degrees apart. Generally, an extremely favorable or helpful aspect.

ZODIAC: The twelve astrological signs. Astrologers think of the heavens as a great circle divided into twelve equal parts, like the face of a clock has its twelve hours. This great circle with its twelve divisions, or signs, is called the Zodiac: Aries the Ram, Taurus the Bull, Gemini the Twins, Cancer the Crab, Leo the Lion, Virgo the Virgin, Libra the Scales, Scorpio the Scorpion, Sagittarius the Archer, Capricorn the Goat, Aquarius the Water-bearer, Pisces the Fish.